THE TABLE THAT SPEAKS
Bringing Communion to Life

THE TABLE THAT SPEAKS
Bringing Communion to Life

Kenneth W. Hagin

16 15 14 13 12 11 10 09   09 08 07 06 05 04 03 02

The Table That Speaks: Bringing Communion to Life
ISBN-13: 978-0-89276-748-9, ISBN-10: 0-89276-748-0

In the U.S. write:
Kenneth Hagin Ministries
P.O. Box 50126
Tulsa, OK 74150-0126
1-888-28-FAITH
www.rhema.org

In Canada write:
Kenneth Hagin Ministries
P.O. Box 335, Station D
Etobicoke (Toronto), Ontario
Canada, M9A 4X3
1-866-70-RHEMA
www.rhemacanada.org

CONTENTS

PREFACE

Why write a book about Communion? Why *read* a book about Communion?

Communion was so important to the Apostle Paul that he told the Corinthian church that many in their congregation were weak and sick, and some had even died, because they were not practicing Communion properly (1 Cor. 11:27–30).

Yet today some Christians may wonder, *Don't we have other subjects that are more vital to study and learn? Is Communion an important topic for today's Church?* Others may view Communion as an archaic ritual that the Church has outgrown, while some may still see Communion as important and practice it, not understanding why they should.

I wrote this book because Communion is one of the most important subjects Christians can study. It's a vital topic for today's Church because the Head of the Church instituted it and commanded us to practice it. Communion isn't an outdated tradition void of meaning and substance. We will never outgrow our need for Communion. As long as we wait for the return of our Lord, Communion will never lose its importance, usefulness, or meaning.

Many preachers have taught that the blood of Jesus still speaks—that it tells a story, the Gospel story. In this book, you are going to discover that the Communion Table also speaks. And the story it tells is just as powerful, eternal, and life-changing as the story the blood tells—because it is the same story.

Our English word *communicate* and the word *communion* both come from the same root word. We communicate something each time we take Communion. The Apostle Paul said, "For as often as ye eat this bread, and drink this cup, ye do shew the Lord's death till he come" (1 Cor. 11:26 *KJV*). Every time we partake of Communion, we show forth, or *proclaim*, the Lord's death until He returns.

Through this book, I want to help believers move beyond a superficial observance of Communion. I want us to actively participate in Communion, knowing why we are doing so. And I want us to participate in faith.

Faith is not something we just "hold on to." God intends that we release our faith, or, as my father Kenneth E. Hagin would say, "turn it loose." Communion offers the perfect opportunity for us to release our faith and receive all that God has provided for us.

We must understand and appropriate all that Jesus had in mind for us when He instituted Communion. As we do, we will receive all that God has made available to us through Christ's redemptive work, and we will effectively demonstrate God's power and blessing to the world.

I pray that the following chapters will help unravel the mystery of the Communion Table and reveal the simple yet powerful truth it holds. We will study what the Table represents; how, when, and why Jesus instituted Communion; how we should approach the Table; and the importance of Communion for our lives today.

Communion is the Table that speaks. I trust that we will all hear its message and in turn share it with the world!

Kenneth W. Hagin

— CHAPTER 1 —

JESUS EAGERLY DESIRED THIS TABLE FOR US

For I received from the Lord what I also passed on to you: The Lord Jesus, on the night he was betrayed, took bread, And when he had given thanks, he broke it and said, "This is my body, which is for you; do this in remembrance of me." In the same way, after supper he took the cup, saying, "This cup is the new covenant in my blood; do this, whenever you drink it, in remembrance of me." For whenever you eat this bread and drink this cup, you proclaim the Lord's death until he comes.

—1 Corinthians 11:23–26

When I was growing up, sometimes my mom and dad, aunts and uncles, and cousins would get together as a family. We'd all sit around the table and there would be plenty of food to eat. We'd all really enjoy ourselves. The adults would sit at the table and talk for hours, and we kids would go outside and play. Besides having plenty of good food, our family gatherings also had plenty of good fellowship.

Sometimes our family would go to my grandmother's house to visit, and she'd cook some of her favorite dishes that we all liked. There would be all kinds of food to eat. During one visit, I remember that people were really eating! It looked to me like things were running out, so I told Grandma, "Everybody's eating up all the food, and I'm not going to get any of your dessert."

She said, "Don't worry, son. There's more in the kitchen."

I want you to understand that at the Lord's Table, there is provision of all kinds. Nothing is lacking. There's plenty on the Lord's Table, and it never runs out! He's got more in the kitchen! He'll just bring it out and put it on the Table. And as we look at the Communion Table in the coming chapters, we'll see what the Lord has provided for us.

First Corinthians 11:23–26 is the Apostle Paul's description of the teaching he received from the Lord Jesus Christ regarding Communion. Although Paul penned this passage, the first instance we see of Communion was actually during the Passover meal Jesus celebrated the night He was betrayed. The Gospels of Matthew, Mark, and Luke all tell of how the Lord instituted Communion at what we call "The Last Supper."

What the Apostle Paul described in First Corinthians 11:23–26 actually took place on the Jewish holiday of Passover. I don't think we can properly understand the Lord's Table until we properly understand the Passover. We'll look more closely at the Jewish Passover a little later.

As we read Luke's account of the Last Supper, I want you to notice that both the Jewish Passover and what we call Communion are in operation. In Luke 22:14–18, Jesus and His disciples are celebrating the Passover, and in verses 19 and 20, Jesus institutes what we call The Lord's Supper, or Communion.

> **LUKE 22:14–20 (*KJV*)**
>
> **14** And when the hour was come, he sat down, and the twelve apostles with him.
>
> **15** And he said unto them, With desire I have desired to eat this passover with you before I suffer:
>
> **16** For I say unto you, I will not any more eat thereof, until it be fulfilled in the kingdom of God.
>
> **17** And he took the cup, and gave thanks, and said, Take this, and divide it among yourselves:
>
> **18** For I say unto you, I will not drink of the fruit of the vine, until the kingdom of God shall come.
>
> **19** And he took bread, and gave thanks, and brake it, and gave unto them, saying, This is my body which is given for you: this do in remembrance of me.
>
> **20** Likewise also the cup after supper, saying, This cup is the new testament in my blood, which is shed for you.

That night as Jesus and His disciples prepared to eat the Passover meal, Jesus told the disciples how much He had been looking forward to sharing that particular Passover with them. Now, let's read verse 15 in the *New King James Version* and the *New International Version*, because I want to highlight Jesus' desire to share this meal with them.

LUKE 22:15 (*NKJV*)

15 Then He said to them, "WITH FERVENT DESIRE I have desired to eat this Passover with you before I suffer."

LUKE 22:15

15 And he said to them, "I HAVE EAGERLY DESIRED to eat this Passover with you before I suffer."

Jesus told His disciples that He was excited about eating that Passover meal with them. He was so excited that He had already reserved a room for their celebration. I want you to notice that this was a special Passover; it had special significance. This was the last meal Jesus was going to share with His disciples before He was taken into custody, treated so cruelly, and ultimately nailed to the Cross. Jesus had planned this Passover meal Himself, and He had prearranged a place for them to share it.

MATTHEW 26:17–18

17 On the first day of the Feast of Unleavened Bread, the disciples came to Jesus and asked, "Where do you want us to make preparations for you to eat the Passover?"

> **18** He replied, "Go into the city to a certain man and tell him, 'The Teacher says: My appointed time is near. I am going to celebrate the Passover with my disciples at your house.'"

Jesus planned to celebrate the Passover with just His disciples. Usually there were multitudes surrounding Him, but this time, there were only He and the Twelve. Where were the throngs of people who had come to Jerusalem to celebrate the Passover? The people who had sung "Hosanna to the Son of David" while waving palm leaves as Jesus rode into Jerusalem were no longer around. Those who had been critical of Him and had claimed that He was a false prophet were not there, nor were those who wanted to take His life.

This Passover meal was a time for close intimate fellowship. It was one last opportunity for Jesus to gather with those who had followed Him so faithfully.

Most likely, however, that night was not the first time that Jesus had celebrated the Passover with His disciples. They probably partook of the Passover together each year as the Law of Moses required.

EXODUS 12:14 (*NKJV*)

> **14** "'So this day shall be to you a memorial; and you shall keep it as a feast to the Lord throughout your generations. You shall keep it as a feast by an everlasting ordinance.'"

Every Jewish person was required by the Law to partake of the Passover. It was a feast to be celebrated yearly by all

Jewish people—an ordinance established by God Himself. The Children of Israel and their descendants were to celebrate the Passover as an ongoing reminder of their deliverance from slavery in Egypt.

The Bible doesn't record the other times Jesus and the disciples celebrated the Passover, but there had to be at least two other occasions, because the disciples followed Jesus as He ministered for three-and-a-half years.

In Matthew 26:17–18, when the disciples asked Jesus where they were going to eat the Passover, Jesus told them where to find the place. If the disciples hadn't celebrated the Passover with Jesus before that time, I believe they wouldn't have been asking. They would have made their own plans. That's another reason why I believe that they had previously partaken of it together. But this time was going to be very special. One last time, Jesus was going to try to help the disciples understand what was about to take place.

On more than one occasion, Jesus had drawn the disciples aside to teach them privately. But there was something different about this time. He sought to prepare His disciples for the trying experiences they were about to face.

Jesus had openly predicted His death on the Cross, but His disciples either were unwilling to believe or did not understand what Jesus was telling them. Perhaps they refused to accept His words about His impending death because they simply could not accept the idea of such a horrible end to His life and ministry. The night of the Last Supper, they were still unconvinced that it was really going to happen, even though Jesus had spoken to them about it.

The disciples were not ready to let Jesus go—not in this manner. They were still looking for Him to establish His kingdom.

LUKE 24:21

21 ". . . but we had hoped that he [Jesus] was the one who was going to redeem Israel. . . ."

According to prophecy, a Deliverer would come to set the Jewish people free from the tyranny of other nations and establish the kingdom of God. And the deliverance of Israel will happen just as surely as prophecy has said! But *that* was not the time, and Jesus didn't come to set up an *earthly* kingdom.

The disciples still didn't understand that Jesus had to die, so Jesus was going to use their last meal together to prepare them for His impending death.

A Last Supper

There is always something special about the last time you fellowship with someone. A meal you share with someone whom you expect to eat with again tomorrow may not seem that special. But if that meal is with someone you will never see again, or won't see for a long time, it is much more significant.

The Passover was always a special occasion for Jesus and His disciples because of what it represented. This time, the meal had extra significance. Jesus reminded His disciples, through the celebration of the Passover Feast, of God's saving grace and power in delivering their forefathers from bondage in Egypt.

EXODUS 12:12-14 (*KJV*)

12 For I will pass through the land of Egypt this night, and will smite all the firstborn in the land of Egypt, both man and beast; and against all the gods of Egypt I will execute judgment: I am the Lord.

13 And the blood shall be to you for a token upon the houses where ye are: and WHEN I SEE THE BLOOD, I WILL PASS OVER YOU, and the plague shall not be upon you to destroy you, when I smite the land of Egypt.

14 And this day shall be unto you for a memorial; and ye shall keep it a feast to the Lord throughout your generations; ye shall keep it a feast by an ordinance for ever.

Passover has always been a special occasion for Jewish people. They ate their first Passover meal on the eve of their release from slavery in Egypt. On that particular occasion, the Lord told them they were to kill a spotless lamb and apply its blood to the top and sides of their doors. Then they were to roast the meat and prepare the meal in a certain way. They were commanded to mark the Passover every year with a special meal, a special commemoration. And many Jewish people still celebrate the Passover today.

In that first Passover, the blood of the lamb was applied to the top and sides of the door so that the death angel would see the blood and *pass over* the Israelites. In other words, no destruction would come to those who were "under the blood."

As we look at this, we can see why Jesus eagerly desired to celebrate this Passover with His disciples. He—the sinless Lamb—was about to pour out His own blood to pay for the sins of His disciples and all mankind. Those who were "under the blood" of Jesus would be freed from slavery to sin. Through Jesus' sacrifice, they would be freed from the clutches of the Destroyer—Satan. No wonder Jesus fervently desired to eat this meal with His disciples. He knew it would symbolize their deliverance! And the Communion Table still speaks to us of our deliverance today!

— CHAPTER 2 —

OUR 'PASSOVER'

As we saw in the last chapter, the Old Testament Passover commemorated the deliverance of the children of Israel, God's people, from the hand of Pharaoh's tyranny in Egypt. In the Bible, Egypt is a type, or symbol, of sin. The Israelites' deliverance required the blood of a lamb. The Communion Table commemorates the believer's spiritual deliverance from the bondage of sin through the blood of the Lord Jesus Christ. Communion could be called a "New Testament Passover."

This so-called New Testament Passover was instituted when the Lord Jesus Christ shared His last meal before the Cross with His disciples. On the Cross, Jesus became the Sacrificial Lamb offered for mankind so that we could be delivered from the tyranny and rule of Satan! Just as the children of Israel observed the Passover to celebrate their deliverance from slavery in Egypt, Christians observe Communion to celebrate deliverance from sin and its consequences. Communion is our "Passover!"

In the Old Testament God said, *"When I see the blood, I will pass over you"* (Exod. 12:13). In other words, when the death angel saw the blood on the door, he *passed over* the people in that house. Friend, I want you to understand that when we accept Jesus Christ as our Savior, the blood of Jesus is applied to our lives. Therefore, when judgment comes our way, it passes over us because of the blood!

Hundreds of years after Israel's release from bondage, Jesus and His disciples were in the Upper Room celebrating what happened that night long ago in Egypt. And Jesus instituted the Lord's Supper as an ordinance for the Church.

Actually, the Lord's Supper is one of the two ordinances of the Church Age of which you and I are a part. The other is water baptism. The time we're living in now is a part of the Church Age, also called the Dispensation of Grace or the Dispensation of Promise. In other times, under other dispensations, different ordinances were to be kept.

The night of His arrest, Jesus instituted the Lord's Supper. And the Apostle Paul said that the Lord taught him about it many years later (see 1 Cor. 11:23).

Notice the importance of what Jesus did. He instituted Holy Communion not for the Jews or the Gentiles but for the Church— the Body of Christ. Every Christian is a member of Christ's Body. The Lord's Supper is an ordinance for *us* to keep.

Have you ever noticed that the Bible deals with three groups of people? The Jews, the Gentiles, and the Church. This ordinance is for the Church—born-again believers in the Lord Jesus Christ. Not just a *local* church, but the universal Church, the *ecclesia*—which means "the called-out ones."

Paul said that he had received the ordinance of Communion from the Lord. And he preached it as part of the Gospel. In his letters, Paul testified that what he preached and taught was not from man.

GALATIANS 1:11–12

11 I want you to know, brothers, that the gospel I preached is not something that man made up.

12 I did not receive it from any man, nor was I taught it; rather, I received it by revelation from Jesus Christ.

Jesus Himself revealed the Gospel to Paul. The apostle used similar words in First Corinthians 11:23–26. He started out by saying, *"For I RECEIVED FROM THE LORD what I also passed on to you."*

Jesus gave this revelation about Communion to Paul so Paul would teach it to the Church. The fact that Jesus revealed this teaching to Paul shows how important Communion is for us today.

The Passover Was Prophetic

In the Old Testament, the Passover was prophetic. Through the centuries, the prophecy had been passed down from generation to generation that there would come a great Deliverer—a Messiah—who would again free the Israelites from their slavery. But, unknown to them, the fulfillment of that prophecy required the death of the Lord Jesus Christ.

At the Last Supper, as Jesus and His disciples celebrated their forefathers' freedom, Jesus picked up the cup and said, *"'Drink from it, all of you. This is my blood of the covenant, which is poured out for many for the forgiveness of sins'"* (Matt. 26:27–28). He was refering to His own blood soon to be shed. Therefore, when we take Communion, we drink from the cup not only to indicate that His blood was shed, but we also drink from the cup to illustrate that the blood must be applied to our hearts. When the blood of Jesus is applied to our hearts, our sins are washed away and we are redeemed.

Now it is important that we understand what Jesus was doing. When Jesus personally took bread and broke it, and He took the cup and drank from it, *He* knew what He was doing. When Jesus instituted Communion with His disciples, I don't think *His disciples* fully understood the significance of His words and actions. It wasn't until later, after all the events of the Cross had unfolded, that they would really grasp the significance of the Lord's Supper.

Jesus understood that His breaking the bread was a type, or shadow, of His offering His own body to be mutilated, beaten, and pierced. When Jesus offered His disciples the cup, it represented His blood being poured out.

As Jesus and His disciples ate the Passover meal, He told them, "I say unto you, I will not any more eat thereof, until it be fulfilled in the kingdom of God" (Luke 22:16 *KJV*). After saying this about His death, Jesus looked at the 12 men who had walked with Him and had been with Him through thick and thin. He saw the troubled looks on their faces, and I believe He understood their heartache.

Jesus tried to explain the coming events to His disciples, but they wouldn't receive what He was saying. Notice, however, that Jesus didn't get upset with them over their lack of understanding. But rather, He continued to encourage, minister to, and instruct them.

Jesus did His best to share with His disciples, to give them strength, encouragement, and hope that would sustain them through the coming hours. Jesus knew that His disciples would be tested to the limit. He understood that they were about to face the most trying three days of their lives. According to the Scriptures, when Jesus was arrested, the disciples ran away (Matt. 26:56). Even Peter, who had said, "Even if I have to die with You, I will not deny You" (Matt. 26:35 *NKJV*), stood in the courtyard outside the high priest's house and said, "I don't even know who this man is!" (Luke 22:54–62).

For the Joy That Was Set Before Him

Jesus was aware of the pain and sorrow the disciples were going to face. Yet He said, *"I have EAGERLY DESIRED to eat this Passover with you . . ."* (Luke 22:15). Jesus anticipated this time, and his death, with great expectation.

Why was Jesus so eager to eat this meal with His disciples? Becauses at the end of that Passover meal He would institute a new "Passover" which we call the Lord's Supper, or Communion, and it would be a symbol of mankind's redemption from slavery to sin. Jesus looked forward to the future with expectation because He knew His death would deliver mankind from the chains of sin, sickness, and poverty forever!

Jesus looked forward to fulfilling the will of God in the earth, even though it meant His death on Calvary.

HEBREWS 12:2

2 Let us fix our eyes on Jesus, the author and perfecter of our faith, who FOR THE JOY SET BEFORE HIM endured the cross, scorning its shame, and sat down at the right hand of the throne of God.

Jesus eagerly awaited the Cross that stood before Him because He understood the message of salvation that the Cross would preach for centuries to come. He looked toward His impending death with hope and anticipation, because He knew that He was the Sacrificial Lamb for all mankind. But He also looked beyond His death, down through time, to when He would come again to earth.

Notice the tone in which the ordinance of the Lord's Supper was established. Jesus and His disciples were giving thanks to God for their forefathers' deliverance from bondage in Egypt. The atmosphere was one of joy, thanksgiving, and celebration.

Yet in the midst of the celebration, Jesus did not hide the sad fact that He was leaving soon. He predicted His death to prepare the disciples for what would happen. Earlier He had even pointed to the way in which He would die.

LUKE 18:31–33

31 Jesus took the Twelve aside and told them, "We are going up to Jerusalem, and everything that is written by the prophets about the Son of Man will be fulfilled.

32 He will be turned over to the Gentiles. They will mock him, insult him, spit on him, flog him and kill him.

33 On the third day he will rise again."

LUKE 22:14–16 (*NKJV*)

14 When the hour had come, He sat down, and the twelve apostles with Him.

15 Then He said to them, "With fervent desire I have desired to eat this Passover with you BEFORE I SUFFER;

16 for I say to you, I will no longer eat of it until it is fulfilled in the kingdom of God."

Jesus told His disciples He would suffer. He understood suffering. He had already suffered much at the hands of His enemies and critics. His own brothers did not respect Him. He had been rejected by people in His hometown, in Jerusalem, and in other cities. The religious leaders had tried to take His life, but He had slipped from their midst to safety (John 10:31,39). They tried to destroy His character by testing and challenging Him. But Jesus stood His ground, spoke the Word of God, and met every challenge!

Jesus *spoke* the Word because He *is* the Word! The Bible says the Word became flesh and dwelt among us (John 1:14). When Jesus was here on earth, He spoke the Word. Although He was the Divine Word, He overcame in His humanity by *speaking* the Word of God. And you and I now have the opportunity to speak the Word too.

We have the *written* Word of God, which the Greek language generally refers to as the *logos*. And the Greek word *rhema* means "spoken word." So when we speak God's Word or make a confession based on His Word, it becomes the *rhema* Word of God just as when Jesus spoke it Himself.

Because of the joy that was set before Him, Jesus refused to focus on the suffering awaiting Him. Instead, He looked forward with hope, knowing the final outcome, and He encouraged His disciples to do the same.

> **JOHN 14:1-3 (*NKJV*)**
>
> **1** "LET NOT YOUR HEART BE TROUBLED; you believe in God, believe also in Me.
>
> **2** In My Father's house are many mansions; if it were not so, I would have told you. I GO TO PREPARE A PLACE FOR YOU.
>
> **3** And if I go and prepare a place for you, I WILL COME AGAIN and receive you to Myself; that where I am, there you may be also."

Notice the encouraging words of hope Jesus gave to His disciples. As He prepared to go to the Cross, He set His mind and heart not on His impending death but on the great day when He will return for us. He was in a paradoxical situation. That Passover was a night of farewell, but by instituting the ordinance of Communion, Jesus established a way for us to see that night as the dawning of a new day—the day of our deliverance!

Jesus' words in Luke 22:16 would be forever stamped upon His disciples' minds. Jesus said that He would not eat another

Passover meal until that day when it would be fulfilled in the Kingdom of God. His words would continually remind the disciples of God's saving grace, power, and promise.

I believe that Jesus was referring to the Marriage Supper of the Lamb (Rev. 19:9), when the whole family of God from throughout the ages will gather together with Jesus to live with Him for eternity.

But there is no eternity in Heaven without the prophecy of the Passover. There is no eternity with God unless you understand that the Communion Table prophesies our deliverance from the bondage of sin. And our deliverance required Jesus' death.

Christ Suffered for Us

When the hour finally arrived, Jesus was beaten, mocked, and scorned as all the forces of hell unleashed their power against Him. Picture in your mind Jesus standing in the judgment hall with the crown of thorns upon His head, blood streaming down His forehead onto His beard and dripping onto the floor, and his back cut to ribbons from the stripes that had been laid upon Him. There He stood, condemned to death, so that we might have life and have it more abundantly (John 10:10).

Jesus *chose* to walk up Golgotha's hill. He had said, "I lay down My life. No man takes it from Me" (John 10:17–18). Jesus went to the Cross willingly. And with three nails and two rough pieces of lumber, He built a bridge whereby mankind could pass from death to life—from the slavery of sin to the freedom of glorious salvation!

Imagine Jesus dying on the Cross, nails in His hands and feet and blood pouring from His body, as He carried the sin of all mankind upon His shoulders. In bitter anguish He looked up to Heaven and cried out, "My God, my God, why hast thou forsaken Me?" (Matt. 27:46 *KJV*).

I believe Jesus suffered the greatest sorrow when God hid His face from Him (Isa. 59:2). For that brief moment, God could not look upon Him because He had made Jesus to be sin for us (2 Cor. 5:21). As Jesus cried out in anguish, the words of the great prophet Isaiah were being fulfilled.

ISAIAH 53:3–5 (*NKJV*)

3 He is despised and rejected by men, a Man of sorrows and acquainted with grief. And we hid, as it were, our faces from Him; He was despised, and we did not esteem Him.

4 Surely He has borne our griefs and carried our sorrows; yet we esteemed Him stricken, smitten by God, and afflicted.

5 But He was wounded for our transgressions, He was bruised for our iniquities; the chastisement for our peace was upon Him, and by His stripes we are healed.

Events had come to pass as Isaiah had prophesied. The Cross was no surprise to Jesus. It's what He came for! Jesus knew from the beginning that the Cross was coming. But the Cross *was* a surprise to His followers. Jesus died a tragic, traumatic death, but it was for a purpose—that we could have life and have it more abundantly (John 10:10).

Jesus' death on the Cross was God's divine plan to deliver mankind from Satan. Satan had walked into God's Garden and had stolen man from Him. God had to pay a ransom to buy man back, and that ransom was the death of His Son Jesus on the Cross. With His death, Jesus paid the ultimate price and made the supreme sacrifice. But He arose! God Himself planned the Cross so that He could ransom us, make us whole, and give us everything that He says belongs to us!

Did you see the movie *The Passion of the Christ*? That was a very good depiction of what happened to Jesus. Although some people said the movie was too gory, I believe that it did not depict the true severity of what Jesus went through for us.

There's an old book that has been out of print for a long time written by Cunningham Geikie, *The Life and Words of Christ*.[1] This book gives an even more detailed description of the suffering and torture that Jesus endured. In his book, Geikie describes the beatings inflicted by the ancient Roman soldiers.

Some of the whips the Romans used were made of several strips of leather with pieces of lead and sharp bone embedded in the ends. According to Geikie, during a beating the whip would often wrap around the victim's body and rip open his chest or stomach—or tear the flesh from his face. Often, victims of Roman floggings did not survive.

Historians describe what a person looked like after a Roman beating such as the one Jesus endured, and the descriptions support what we read in Isaiah chapter 52.

ISAIAH 52:14

14 . . . There were many who were appalled at him—his appearance was so disfigured beyond that of any man and his form marred beyond human likeness.

The Amplified Bible says that Jesus became an object of horror and many were astonished at Him. I'm going to say it in modern language: Jesus was so mutilated that He was not even recognizable.

Friend, Jesus took that excruciating beating *for us.* When He allowed those soldiers to bind, club, slap, pound, kick, spit on, whip, and stab Him—He did it *for us.* And He carried His own cross and endured the agony and disgrace of crucifixion *for us.*

When we come to the Communion Table, if we will listen and understand, we will hear it speaking to us of its origins in the Jewish Passover, which commemorated the deliverance of the children of Israel from slavery in Egypt. In the first Passover, a lamb without blemish was slain, and its blood was applied to the doors of Jewish homes. But we will also hear the Table speak of *our* deliverance. Jesus, the spotless Lamb of God, was slain for our salvation, and His blood has been applied to our hearts. The Table speaks to us of our own "Passover" celebration: the ordinance of Communion.

---

[1] Cunningham Geikie, *The Life and Words of Christ* (New York: American Book Exchange, 1880), 768–769.

— Chapter 3 —

Examining the
Elements of Communion

For I received from the Lord Himself that which I passed on to you [it was given to me personally], that the Lord Jesus on the night when He was treacherously delivered up and while His betrayal was in progress took bread,

And when He had given thanks, He broke [it] and said, Take, eat. This is My body, which is broken for you. Do this to call Me [affectionately] to remembrance.

Similarly when supper was ended, He took the cup also, saying, This cup is the new covenant [ratified and established] in My blood. Do this, as often as you drink [it], to call Me [affectionately] to remembrance.

For every time you eat this bread and drink this cup, you are representing and signifying and proclaiming the fact of the Lord's death until He comes [again].

—1 Corinthians 11:23–26 (*Amplified*)

In this chapter I want us to examine the actual *elements* of the Communion Table—the bread and the cup, or, symbolically speaking, the body and blood of our Lord Jesus.

As Paul reminded us in First Corinthians 11:23–26, Jesus took bread, gave thanks, broke it, and said, "This is My body, which is broken for you." Then He took the cup, gave thanks, drank, and said, "This cup is the new covenant in My blood."

The bread symbolizes Jesus' body that was broken for us. Today, many churches use wafers to celebrate Communion, but when I was a kid, we used bits of saltine crackers. If the church didn't have crackers, they just took a loaf of bread and pinched it into many little pieces. It doesn't matter what type of bread you use because the bread is simply a representation, or symbol, of the Lord's body.

We break the bread or serve it in pieces to remind us that Jesus' body was battered for our physical healing. First Peter 2:24 says, "*. . . by his wounds you have been healed.*" On his own, man could never escape the clutches of disease. But God allowed His Son, Jesus Christ, to receive stripes upon His back for the healing of all mankind. We acknowledge and celebrate our healing when we partake of the bread during Communion.

The cup is a symbol of the blood that Jesus shed for us on the Cross. The juice we drink during Communion symbolizes the blood that was poured out to cleanse us and redeem us from sin.

Christ: The Bread of Life

First, I want to call your attention to the Communion element that we call "the bread." At times it seems in some circles that the bread takes a back seat to the cup in the Communion setting. But the bread is just as significant as the cup. You can't separate the two. They work together. It's similar to your physical body in the sense that you can't separate your blood from your body and still be a living organism. It takes both the body and the blood for you to be alive.

We have to purpose in our hearts to always give as much importance to the bread as we do the cup in the Communion ceremony because both of them represent the same thing—the Lord Jesus Christ.

The Bible mentions several types of bread, and we're going to look at each of them to see what they have in common with Communion.

Natural Bread

When Jesus taught the disciples to pray, "Give us this day our daily bread" (Matt. 6:11 *KJV*), He was talking about *natural bread*, or natural food that we eat to sustain our physical body. Many times when the Bible talks about bread, it simply means food in general, not just bread.

God designed our body in such a way that we need to eat food regularly to sustain it. Some people eat natural food simply out of necessity. They're not really hungry but they know they need to eat to keep up their strength. If we abstain from natural food for a long time, we will die of starvation. We must have natural food in order to live.

We know that a little Communion wafer cannot sustain anyone physically. But just as eating natural food is a necessary part of our physical life, partaking of Communion is a necessary part of our Christian life. The Bible is careful to point out that we need to feed our spirit as well as our body. That's exactly what Jesus told the devil when he tempted Him to use His supernatural power to create food for Himself.

MATTHEW 4:1-4

1 Then Jesus was led by the Spirit into the desert to be tempted by the devil.

2 After fasting for forty days and forty nights, he was hungry.

3 The tempter came to him and said, "If you are the Son of God, tell these stones to become bread."

4 Jesus answered, "It is written: 'Man does not live on bread alone, but on every word that comes from the mouth of God.'"

Jesus had been fasting for more than a month, and He was hungry. (You would be too!) So the devil tempted Jesus to make Himself something to eat. But in Matthew 4:4, Jesus said that we must have more than natural bread—we need to feed our spirit on God's Word. Prayer and partaking of Communion also strengthen our faith and provide us with spiritual nourishment and refreshment.

Miracle Bread

I want to look at two instances in the Bible when God provided *miracle bread*. The first time was when the Israelites grumbled for food to eat in the desert and God supplied them with manna.

EXODUS 16:14–15

14 When the dew was gone, thin flakes like frost on the ground appeared on the desert floor.

15 When the Israelites saw it, they said to each other, "What is it?" For they did not know what it was. Moses said to them, "It is the bread the Lord has given you to eat."

The Israelites had no other way to get food while they wandered in the desert, so God sent them bread from Heaven. No matter where they wandered in the wilderness, they were cared for as God supernaturally provided manna for them for 40 years.

Hundreds of years later, we see another time God miraculously provided bread for His people. In Matthew 14:17–21, Jesus and His disciples were trying to get away privately to rest for a while, but the crowds followed them. Jesus had compassion on the crowds and healed the sick. Then He taught the people.

As evening approached, the disciples urged Jesus to send the people away so they could get something to eat. But Jesus said, "You feed them."

MATTHEW 14:17–21

17 "We have here only five loaves of bread and two fish," they answered.

18 "Bring them here to me," he [Jesus] said.

19 And he directed the people to sit down on the grass. Taking the five loaves and the two fish and looking up to heaven, he gave thanks and broke the loaves. Then he gave them to the disciples, and the disciples gave them to the people.

20 They all ate and were satisfied, and the disciples picked up twelve basketfuls of broken pieces that were left over.

21 The number of those who ate was about five thousand men, besides women and children.

Jesus took the loaves and the fish, gave thanks for them, and had the disciples distribute them to the people. More than 5,000 men, women, and children ate and were satisfied, and there were 12 baskets of leftovers!

When you're in the wilderness and there is nothing but lack on every side, if you will trust God, He will miraculously supply whatever it is you need. Don't be fearful about your food supply. God took care of His children a long time ago, and He can take care of you now!

Some people say, "That's sort of simplistic." Well, I'm just simple enough to believe what the Bible says. God still works miracles today. His miracle supply has not run out. He still has plenty to go around. Even after He has blessed us so many times and has given so much to so many, His storehouse is still full and running over! The Communion Table should remind us that because of what Jesus has done for us, God will supply whatever we need.

Showbread

Showbread, or the bread of the Presence, is the third type of bread we're going to look at. The showbread was placed on the golden table in the Holy Place of the Tabernacle and in the Temple at Jerusalem.

LEVITICUS 24:5–8

5   "Take fine flour and bake twelve loaves of bread, using two-tenths of an ephah for each loaf.

6   Set them in two rows, six in each row, on the table of pure gold before the Lord.

7   Along each row put some pure incense as a memorial portion to represent the bread and to be an offering made to the Lord by fire.

8   This bread is to be set out before the Lord regularly, Sabbath after Sabbath, on behalf of the Israelites, as a lasting covenant."

The showbread symbolized God's constant presence with His people and that He always provided for them. The showbread was offered to the Lord every Sabbath as a lasting covenant.

Under the New Covenant, we know God is always with us because He said He would never leave nor forsake us (Heb. 13:5), and He promised to supply our every need according to His glorious riches in Christ Jesus (Phil. 4:19). I want you to understand that the Communion Table represents the everlasting covenant between Jesus Christ and God the Father. Those of us who have accepted Jesus as Savior are "in Christ" and share in that covenant. Every time we partake of Communion, we reaffirm that covenant.

Unleavened Bread

The fourth type of bread we're going to study is *unleavened bread*. This is bread made without yeast. It is the type of bread that was designated to be used during the Passover.

EXODUS 12:17

17 "Celebrate the Feast of Unleavened Bread, because it was on this very day that I brought your divisions out of Egypt. Celebrate this day as a lasting ordinance for the generations to come."

When God established the Feast of Unleavened Bread, He gave the Israelites a type or shadow of that which was to come. He told His people to celebrate the Feast of Unleavened Bread as a lasting symbol of their deliverance from the bondage of slavery. Then hundreds of years later, on the night when He instituted what we call The Lord's Supper, Jesus told us to celebrate Communion as a lasting symbol of our deliverance from bondage to sin and death.

Living Bread

The last type of bread we're going to look at is the *Living Bread*. In John 6:51 Jesus said, *"I am the living bread that came down from heaven. If anyone eats of this bread, he will live forever. This bread is my flesh, which I will give for the life of the world."*

Jesus called Himself the Living Bread. In other places in the New Testament, Jesus referred to Himself as the Bread of Life, the Bread of God, and the True Bread from Heaven. All these titles indicate for us a whole new dimension of life that we did not know about and could not experience until Christ came and gave Himself for us. We partake of the Living Bread when we accept Jesus Christ as our personal Savior.

JOHN 6:48–50

48 I [Jesus] am the bread of life.

49 Your forefathers ate the manna in the desert, yet they died.

50 But here is the bread that comes down from heaven, which a man may eat and not die.

Jesus pointed out that God gave the Israelites *natural* bread to eat in the desert and they still died. But Jesus came as the *spiritual* bread, and when we "eat" this bread, it gives us eternal life. Jesus wasn't saying that we wouldn't die a natural death, because we know that, should He tarry His coming, we will die physically. He was saying that when we receive Him we receive everlasting life, and we will not die *spiritually.*

Christ is the spiritual bread sent from Heaven. Natural bread is earthly, but spiritual bread is heavenly. Natural bread is corruptible, but spiritual bread is incorruptible. Natural bread is limited, but spiritual bread is unlimited. Natural bread feeds the body. Spiritual bread feeds the spirit of man.

The Bread Was Broken for Our Healing

When Jesus instituted Communion, He used the bread to represent how His body would be battered, beaten, and bruised to pay the price for our healing.

1 PETER 2:24 (*KJV*)

24 Who his own self bare our sins in his own body on the tree, that we, being dead to sins, should live unto righteousness: by whose stripes ye were healed.

Without Jesus Christ taking the stripes upon His back, there would be no healing. We would be lost and undone, sick and afflicted. Thank God that Jesus bore those stripes upon His back, because those stripes bought our healing!

The bread or wafer that we eat during the Communion service represents the Living Bread Who walked upon the earth and went about teaching, preaching, healing, and doing good (Acts 10:38). Jesus' body was beaten and broken, hung on a cross, and put in a grave. But remember—Jesus is the *Living* Bread! He is life everlasting, so the grave could not hold Him!

Most religions can point to marked graves where their leaders are buried. Those tombs are still sealed and the bodies still buried, because there is only one Living Bread. There is only one tomb that is now empty. It stands empty because Jesus Christ, our Living Bread, rose from the grave! And because He lives, we can live (John 14:19)!

I hope you have a better understanding of the bread of the Communion Table. So many times the bread of Communion is treated as an afterthought. Friend, it is not an afterthought. It is as much a part of Communion as the cup.

The bread of the Communion Table reminds us that we need to eat spiritual food as well as natural food. It tells us that God has met needs miraculously in the past, and He will do it again when we take Him at His Word. The Communion bread declares that God is always with us and has promised to meet all our needs. It proclaims to us that Jesus' sacrifice has freed us forever from bondage to sin. And it states that Jesus' broken body paid the price for our healing.

The bread of the Communion Table speaks to us of these blessings of God every time we celebrate The Lord's Supper.

The Blood of the Lamb

I want to look now at the Communion element we call "the cup." As we've seen, the cup of the Communion Table symbolizes the blood of Jesus that was shed at Calvary for the remission of our sins. There is not much teaching on the blood these days. When I was a boy growing up in Pentecostal churches, we used to hear a lot of teaching about the blood. And we used to hear people plead the blood of Jesus over situations in life, because the blood of the Lord Jesus Christ protects us! (We'll look at this more later.)

There's Redeeming Power in the Blood

In the Church of today, many people don't want to talk about the blood of Jesus. In fact, in some modern hymnals, songs that have anything to do with the blood have been removed because those songs are considered "too gory." Some people even say it's not politically correct to talk about the blood of Jesus. But that's just one more way the devil tries to stifle the Christian, because there is wonder-working power in the blood!

Many of the songs we sing about the blood have tremendous significance. For example, look at the words of this old hymn: "There is a fountain filled with blood drawn from Immanuel's veins; And sinners, plunged beneath that flood, lose all their guilty stains."[1] That song speaks of the cleansing power of the blood. We would never be cleansed from sin without the shed blood of Jesus Christ. The blood of Jesus wipes our sin away and washes us white as snow.

MATTHEW 26:28

28 This is my blood of the covenant, which is poured out for many for the forgiveness of sins.

We need to remember that the blood Jesus shed on Calvary is the reason we have salvation, because the Scriptures say that without the shedding of blood, there is no remission, or forgiveness, of sin (Heb. 9:22). The blood is worth talking about—and worth celebrating!

God sent His Son to die on the Cross for the sins of humanity. He sent Jesus to Calvary so that we could be delivered from sin, condemnation, sickness, poverty, and all that goes along with spiritual death. Jesus' death was the only way we could be redeemed. It was impossible for man to redeem himself. But what man cannot do, God can (Luke 18:27)!

Man cannot save himself, but God sent His only Son to bring salvation to mankind. Man could never remove the verdict of "guilty sinner," nor the sentence of eternal separation from God. But God sent His Son to make us righteous. Being made "righteous" means we now have right standing with God. We are no longer separated from God by sin. We are reconciled to God and have come into right standing with Him by accepting Jesus Christ as Savior. The blood of Jesus was spilled at Calvary for our salvation and our sin was completely blotted out.

In the Old Testament, the children of Israel had to offer the blood of bulls, lambs, and goats to *cover up* their sin. The animals they offered had to be without spot or blemish. In other words, they had to be perfect. Leviticus chapter 16 gives explicit instructions about these sacrifices and what was to happen on the Day of Atonement.

The first thing the priest had to do on that day was make a sin offering for himself and his household. Then he would cast lots for two goats. One would be the sin offering for the people and the other would be the scapegoat.

The priest would kill the first goat, then take its blood and sprinkle it on the mercy seat and on the horns of the altar. Then he would lay his hands on the head of the live goat and confess the sins of the Israelites, symbolically putting their sins on the goat's head. The goat became their substitute when the priest transferred their sins onto it. The goat would symbolically carry away all the sins of the people. Under the Law of Moses, this process was repeated once each year.

Then one fateful day the blood of God's perfect Sacrifice was shed—once and for all—as Jesus Christ hung suspended between Heaven and earth on that cruel cross on Golgotha's hill. Jesus' blood flowed out from under the crown of thorns on His head, from the stripes on His back, from the nails in His hands and feet, and from the wound where the spear was thrust into His side.

Before Jesus' death, many animals had been slain to atone for sin. Jesus was the last Sacrifice that God required. Jesus didn't merely *atone* for our sins; He washed them away! Jesus became the Supreme Sacrifice and sinless Substitute for all mankind when the sin of the world was transferred onto Him once and for all.

2 CORINTHIANS 5:21

21 God made him who had no sin to be sin for us, so that in him we might become the righteousness of God.

It's very important that you understand that *Jesus did not sin.* But the Word of God says *He was made to be sin* for us. Jesus poured out His blood at Calvary as He died in our place. But Jesus didn't just die. He also arose! He ascended into Heaven and carried His blood to the Father on High to make a way for

you and me to receive salvation and right standing with God
(see Heb. 9:8–14).

There's Protection in the Blood

We've just considered the *cleansing* power of the blood of the
Lamb. There is also *protecting* power in Jesus' blood.

Looking back to the origin of Passover, God promised that
when He saw the lamb's blood on the doorposts of the Israelites'
homes, the death angel would pass over them.

EXODUS 12:12–13 (*KJV*)

12 For I will pass through the land of Egypt this
night, and will smite all the firstborn in the land
of Egypt, both man and beast; and against all
the gods of Egypt I will execute judgment: I am
the Lord.

13 And the blood shall be to you for a token
upon the houses where ye are: and WHEN I SEE
THE BLOOD, I WILL PASS OVER YOU, and the
plague shall not be upon you to destroy you,
when I smite the land of Egypt.

According to these verses, the blood from the natural lamb
provided protection for the children of Israel. In the same way,
there is protecting power in the blood of Jesus for God's people
today.

The blood of the Lamb acts as a seal placed upon us. That
seal provides us with many things—and divine protection is
one of them!

The President of the United States seals documents with the presidential seal. When he affixes that seal on a document, it means the document is backed by all the powers of the United States of America.

Jesus Christ shed His blood on Calvary to cleanse us and redeem us from sin. When we accepted Him as our Savior, He affixed or applied His blood to our hearts and sealed us with a holy seal. Now all the power of Heaven stands behind that seal!

The cup on the Communion Table represents the blood that Jesus poured out for us at Calvary. His blood cleansed us from sin. And just as the blood of lambs protected the children of Israel—causing the death angel to pass over their homes the night they were delivered from slavery in Egypt—so the blood of Jesus can protect God's people today. Because of the cup and what it represents, the Communion Table speaks to us of forgiveness for our sins and protection for all of us who are part of the Body of Christ.

The elements of Communion—the bread and the cup—still speak to us of the body and blood of the Lord. They are a living reminder that Jesus laid down his life for us and, through His sacrifice, provided for us all the benefits of salvation.

---

[1] William Cowper, "There Is a Fountain Filled With Blood."

— CHAPTER 4 —

WHY DO WE CELEBRATE COMMUNION?

The teaching I gave you was given me personally by the Lord himself, and it was this: the Lord Jesus, in the same night in which he was betrayed, took bread and when he had given thanks he broke it and said, "This is my body—and it is for you. Do this in remembrance of me." Similarly, when supper was ended, he took the cup saying, "This cup is the new agreement made by my blood: do this, whenever you drink it, in remembrance of me." This can only mean that whenever you eat this bread and drink this cup, you are proclaiming the Lord's death until he comes again.

—1 Corinthians 11:23–26 (*Phillips*)

When the Lord called me to start RHEMA Bible Church, He dealt with me about the significance of Holy Communion. He said, "If you're going to have Communion, then make Communion the focus of the whole service." So I've always tried to preach a message that involves the Communion Table whenever we serve Communion.

Whether you call it Communion, the Lord's Supper, the Lord's Table, or the Eucharist, this ceremony is a holy memorial symbolic of Jesus' death. It's also a celebration of all that His death, burial, and resurrection have brought us. But in some churches, Communion is treated as a byproduct or an afterthought. I grew up in a church like that. Communion was tacked on to the end of the church service. We would be almost ready to dismiss and someone would say, "It's time for Communion."

Many people come from churches and theological backgrounds where Communion is nothing more than a ritual. They took Communion, but it was just something they did—the ceremony didn't have the meaning or significance for them that it should have. As a result, many church people wonder why we take Communion at all. That is one of the reasons for this book. In this chapter, I want to explain why we celebrate Holy Communion.

Communion Is an Ordinance

The first reason we celebrate Communion is because *Jesus established it as an ordinance.* In other words, He commanded us to do it. In Luke 22:19, Jesus told His disciples, *"Do this in remembrance of me.*" And in First Corinthians 11:23–26, Jesus used the same words two more times when He taught Paul about Communion. Jesus instructed us to take Communion in remembrance of Him. Therefore, we take Communion in obedience to the Lord.

Jesus said, *"If you love me, you will obey what I command"* (John 14:15). If we love the Lord, we will do what He said. Every individual believer and all of us as a corporate body of believers should come to the Table in loving obedience to the command of the Lord Jesus Christ.

Partaking of Communion is not something we are to do only if we want to. Jesus said, "Do this," so we should obey. But when we partake of the bread and the cup, we should do so out of a heart filled with love and thanksgiving for the Lord and what He has done for us.

Communion Is a Tradition

The second reason we should partake of Communion is that *it's a tradition* of the apostolic times. When the Charismatic renewal started in the early 1970s, many Charismatic churches did away with Communion altogether. They saw it as just another church tradition.

Not all traditions are bad. Some church traditions are good for us to keep. We have to judge them according to the Word of God.

The apostles observed Communion. They partook of Communion the night Jesus initiated it, and they continued to do so because He told them to.

Some people have said that the Lord's Supper was just for Jesus' original 12 apostles. But the Apostle Paul said, *"For I received from the Lord what I also passed on to you . . ."* (1 Cor. 11:23). Paul said that he had received teaching about Communion from the Lord. Paul wasn't present when Jesus initiated The Lord's Supper. But Jesus taught him about it. And then Paul taught us—the grafted-in branch, the believing Gentiles—so that we could enjoy the provisions of the Table. Matthew was present in the Upper Room and wrote about Communion from the experience of being there, but Paul wrote from being personally taught by the Lord.

The Early Church observed Communion regularly and frequently. Some Bible scholars believe that the "breaking of bread" mentioned in Acts 2:42 and 20:7 refers to Communion. As we've seen, we can also read about it in Paul's first letter to the church at Corinth. Paul wrote to the Corinthian believers to instruct them concerning the Lord's Supper. He had to correct them and reinstruct them about how to celebrate Communion, and he had to remind them that Communion was not a time for selfishness and division.

We know that Paul had already taught the Corinthians about Communion because he said, *"For I received from the Lord what I also PASSED ON TO YOU . . ."* (1 Cor. 11:23). "Passed on" is past tense. That means that before Paul wrote them this letter, he had already taught them the proper way to partake of Communion. The members of the Corinthian church were getting together for Communion, but they were not following the instructions for the Lord's Supper that Paul had given them. So Paul wrote to them to set them straight.

1 CORINTHIANS 11:17-22

17 In the following directives I have no praise for you, for your meetings do more harm than good.

18 In the first place, I hear that when you come together as a church, there are divisions among you, and to some extent I believe it.

19 No doubt there have to be differences among you to show which of you have God's approval.

20 When you come together, it is not the Lord's Supper you eat,

21 for as you eat, each of you goes ahead without waiting for anybody else. One remains hungry, another gets drunk.

22 Don't you have homes to eat and drink in? Or do you despise the church of God and humiliate those who have nothing? What shall I say to you? Shall I praise you for this? Certainly not!

Some theologians say that the Early Church held *agape* feasts, or "love feasts," in connection with the Lord's Supper. These would be similar to what some people today call a "potluck dinner." The believers brought food to share with each other. The rich people brought more and the poor brought less, but because of divisions in that church, the rich ate more and the poor were left hungry. People were taking whole platefuls of food and not waiting for everyone to be served before they started eating and drinking, so some of them went hungry while others got drunk (v. 21).

In First Corinthians 11:17–22, the Apostle Paul rebuked the members of the Corinthian church. He said that their meetings were doing more harm than good because those gatherings were stirring up strife among the people. That's why Paul told them, "Don't do it that way. Wait for each other. And if you're hungry, eat before you get to the meeting" (1 Cor. 11:33–34). You see, they were using that holy time to eat dinner and get drunk.

Communion is not a time to come get something to eat. It is a time of unity in the Body of Christ. Communion is a sacred tradition that we should treat with reverence and respect.

Communion Is a Memorial

Another reason we partake of Communion is that *it is a memorial.* A memorial is a special service, tribute, or monument of some kind designed to help others remember a person or group of people, or an event. A memorial service for someone who has died is an example of such an event.

As Americans, we have a number of days on which we memorialize, or honor, people who have had significant impact upon our nation—people such as George Washington, Abraham Lincoln, and Dr. Martin Luther King Jr. On Veteran's Day we honor those who have served or are currently serving our country in the Armed Forces. On Memorial Day we honor those who gave their lives while serving under the banner of the Stars and Stripes.

But in the midst of all our natural celebrations, we need to remember that our freedom and liberty is God's idea, not man's.

God wants us to live free in every sense of the word. He sent Jesus to pay a costly price for our freedom, so we should do everything in our power to stay free. After we've been set free, we must not allow ourselves to become slaves to sin, sickness, poverty, or the yoke of the devil ever again! Freedom is God's idea, and through the memorial of Communion He has given us a way to remember and celebrate the freedom from Satan's power that Jesus purchased for us.

Patriotic holidays in the United States help us remember that the blood of many American soldiers has been spilled on the soil of many lands so that we could live free today. In the same way, the Communion Table reminds us that the blood of the Lord Jesus Christ was shed on Calvary so that we could live eternally free!

God was the original Freedom Fighter. Many American families have sent their children to fight for freedom. But God was the first One to do so, because Jesus was slain from the foundation of the world (Rev. 13:8). God's Son became the Supreme Sacrifice. And because *His* blood was shed on Calvary's hill, you and I have spiritual freedom today.

People like to think that they are free just because they live in a country like America, but no one is really free until he or she is free from the tyranny of sin. A person may be free from the control of a dictator, but that person is not truly free until he has been set free from sin by the blood of the Lord Jesus Christ! Real freedom starts when a person is born again. Knowing Christ is the ultimate freedom. Thank God for the freedom we have in the United States to enjoy life, liberty, and the pursuit of happiness, but ultimate freedom is freedom from the devil's tyranny.

JOHN 8:31–32,36

31 To the Jews who had believed him, Jesus said, "If you hold to my teaching, you are really my disciples.

32 Then you will know the truth, and the truth will set you free. . . ."

36 "So if the Son sets you free, you will be free indeed."

Real freedom only comes when we make Jesus Christ our Lord and Savior. To make Him Lord means to obey His teachings and do what He says to do. When we do that, we are no longer under the rule of Satan. We have put ourselves under the rule of the Father, Jesus Christ, and the Holy Spirit.

Communion brings to mind the spiritual freedom God has enabled us to walk in through Christ. But we must understand that this freedom does not give us a license to do whatever we want to do. Freedom has boundaries. And if we observe those boundaries, we will continue to walk in freedom.

I encourage you to walk in the freedom God intends for each of us to enjoy. But at the Communion Table, as we remember and celebrate our freedom, let us not forget the price that was paid for it. Freedom is not free! Jesus paid for our freedom with His blood.

Each day, we must maintain the freedom that Christ has gained for us. It's one thing to declare war on the devil and gain victory over him. Jesus did that for us. It's another thing *to maintain* our freedom. In that, we have a part to play. We have to fight to maintain our spiritual freedom because the enemy would love to pull us back into bondage to sin, sickness, and lack.

The Communion Table is a memorial, helping us remember our spiritual freedom. The bread and cup bring to our minds the broken body and shed blood of Jesus, which made it possible for us to be truly free. Memorials are important to us in America because they remind us of our nation's history and heritage. The Communion memorial is important to us as Christians because it helps us remember Jesus Christ and all that He did for us.

Every time we hold the Communion bread and cup in our hands, we should remember Jesus, the sacrificial Lamb of God. He died that we might have life. He took stripes upon His back for our physical healing. He shed His blood that we might be redeemed. If there ever was a person who should have a memorial in His honor, it is Jesus Christ!

I'm very proud that I wore the U.S. Army green. And I'm very proud of every person who has worn the uniform of the United States military. They have guaranteed our nation the freedom we have today. I salute them and I thank God for them. But I thank God even more for Jesus Christ!

We get upset—and rightly so—if our soldiers are not honored or our memorials are not treated with respect. But what do we do when Communion is not honored or treated with respect? Jesus did more for us than anyone else who has ever lived. We should treat Him with the honor and respect He deserves!

Jesus Himself set up Communion as a memorial. He said, "Eat the bread and drink the cup in remembrance of Me." We celebrate Communion to memorialize God's redemptive plan that Jesus Christ consummated with His death on Calvary. Communion is a memorial, but this memorial is not some avenue or boulevard named for Jesus Christ. It's not a silent, towering statue or some special day recognized by a nation. It is the ceremony we call Communion. The memorial of the Communion Table shouts, "Jesus died! He was buried! But He arose, and He's coming again!"

Communion Is a Time of Thanksgiving

Another reason we celebrate Communion is that *it's a time of thanksgiving*—an occasion for us to give thanks for what God has done for us through Jesus Christ.

We need to thank God because He gave us Jesus. But we also need to thank Jesus Christ, the Son of God, for willingly laying down His life for us. Jesus said, *"No one takes it* [My life] *from me, but I lay it down of my own accord. I have authority to lay it down and authority to take it up again . . ."* (John 10:18).

Jesus was saying in that verse, "As an act of My will, I give My life so that every man, woman, boy, and girl who has ever lived, and every person who will ever live until I come again, might have life and have it more abundantly." During Communion, we can stop to remember and give thanks for the benefits that are ours because Jesus willingly gave His life.

PSALM 103:2–5 (*KJV*)

2 Bless the Lord, O my soul, and FORGET NOT ALL HIS BENEFITS:

3 Who forgiveth all thine iniquities; who healeth all thy diseases;

4 Who redeemeth thy life from destruction; who crowneth thee with lovingkindness and tender mercies;

5 Who satisfieth thy mouth with good things; so that thy youth is renewed like the eagle's.

This psalm reminds us of several benefits of salvation. God has blessed us with forgiveness of our sins, healing, protection, love, mercy, provision, and strength. Those benefits and so many more are ours. And taking Communion is a way for us to give thanks for all these wonderful benefits Jesus purchased for us with His broken body and shed blood.

Communion Is a Bond of Fellowship

We also celebrate Communion because *it's a bond of fellowship*. Have you ever noticed how much of your bonding and fellowshipping with other people takes place around a table while you're eating? It's common to invite friends and family over for a meal or to go out with them and get something to eat. That's one important way we bond and fellowship with one another!

At the Communion Table, we as believers gather to maintain a bond of fellowship with God. Communion is also a time of blessed fellowship with our brothers and sisters in the Lord, our spiritual family. We are God's family. He has adopted us, so Jesus is our Elder Brother and God is our Heavenly Father. Communion is a time for the family to get together!

At RHEMA Bible Church, we take Communion together as a spiritual family and as natural families. I instruct the people to find where their family members are sitting—even if it's in the choir loft. I include the children in the service as well. I like to have the children partake of Communion because they're also a part of God's family. Looking across the auditorium, I can see natural families gathered together and the entire church body, a spiritual family, fellowshipping together around the Lord's Table.

When my wife and I have a special dinner at our home, we invite the whole family, making sure everyone is present. We invite our children and our children's children! Well, when we have this special celebration time at the Lord's Table, it is only proper and fitting that *all* of the family be there. Children should be taught what we have because of Jesus' death, burial, and resurrection, and they should enjoy the blessings of Communion with us.

We have *open* Communion at our church. In other words, whether you are a member of our church or a visitor, as long as you're born again by the blood of the Lord Jesus Christ, you can partake of Communion with us. We all come together as *the family of God*, not limiting involvement to members of our local church family.

When we come to the Lord's Table and share fellowship with one another, we hold the emblems in our hands until everyone has been served, waiting to partake together as God's family. There are no big "I's" and little "you's," no "rich" and "poor." We're just all there together as a family, rejoicing that God has brought us together to share a bond of fellowship with Him and each other.

Communion Is a Public Profession of Faith and Commitment

We celebrate Communion because *it's a time when we publicly profess our commitment to the Lord Jesus Christ.* You see, there's more to Communion than just eating a wafer or piece of bread and drinking a small cup of juice. It is a time for us to profess our loyalty to the Lord and our commitment to serve Him at all costs.

1 CORINTHIANS 10:16

16 Is not the cup of thanksgiving for which we give thanks a participation in the blood of Christ? And is not the bread that we break a participation in the body of Christ?

Communion is a symbol of our relationship and fellowship with Jesus Christ. By taking Communion, we're declaring to everyone around us that we believe that Jesus died for our sins and that we are committed to living our life for Him.

As we have studied in this chapter, there are many reasons why we celebrate Communion. We come to the Table because Jesus said to come. We come in obedience. We come as His other followers have down through the ages to receive whatever we need from Him. We come to give honor and respect to our Lord. We come to offer our thanks and praise for what Jesus did. We come to unite ourselves in a bond of fellowship with God and with fellow members of His family. And we come to profess our faith in and commitment to Christ.

I hope you now have a better understanding of why we celebrate Communion. So when someone asks you why you do so, you can explain the many powerful and wonderful reasons for the Communion Table.

— Chapter 5 —

How Should We Partake
of Communion?

We've looked at the origins of Communion, the elements of
the bread and cup, and the reasons why it's important for us to
partake of the Lord's Supper. Now I want us to consider how
we partake of the Communion Table. As we'll see, knowing
how we are to partake is just as important as knowing why we
do so.

Participation Is Not Optional

First, we are to actively participate in Communion. Partaking
of Communion is *participation* time for the believer. It is not
spectator time. But what exactly are we participating in? Paul
dealt with this question in his first letter to the Corinthians.

1 CORINTHIANS 10:16

16 Is not the cup of thanksgiving for which we give thanks a participation in the blood of Christ? And is not the bread that we break a participation in the body of Christ?

Paul told us that as we eat the bread and drink the cup, we are participating in worshipping God and fellowshipping with Him. The Greek word translated as "participation" here can also be translated as "communion" or "fellowship."

First Corinthians 10:16 is taken from a letter of correction that Paul wrote to the church at Corinth. The believers there had come out of paganism. There were temples to pagan gods and goddesses all around the city. In First Corinthians chapter 10, Paul addressed the issue of idolatry. In warning the people, he pointed out that when they eat food sacrificed to idols they are participating in worshipping demons. But when they take Communion they are participating in worshipping God because the bread and cup symbolize our fellowship with Christ.

Get Off the Sidelines

We should not come to the Communion Table as spectators; we should come as active participants, because the Word of God says that we are all partakers (1 Cor. 10:17 *KJV*). A partaker is a participant. A spectator is someone who is not participating but is just sitting in the stands watching.

Many people sit in the stands (or in their living room) and watch football games, and they talk about what they would do if they were the quarterback. But most of these people have never been in that position, and some of them have never even played football!

It's one thing to sit in your house in your big, comfortable recliner watching a game and say, "Well, he should have done such and such." But it's another thing to be the quarterback out on the field with the ball cocked behind your ear ready to throw, and you're trying to find a receiver while 300-pound guys are bearing down on you with the sole objective of rubbing you into the ground! If that were you out there, most likely you'd change your way of thinking in a hurry! Two minutes of the real thing, and the next time you watched a game from the comfort of your living room you wouldn't ask, "Why didn't he throw the ball?" or, "How come he threw an interception?" You'd know it was because of the pressure of the situation.

Well, you might be facing a pressure situation in your life today, with the enemy bearing down on you, coming at you from all sides. Instead of sitting down on the sidelines, you need to stand tall and say, "I remember what the Word of God says about the Communion Table. I remember that the Table is about salvation, redemption, protection, healing, deliverance, and provision. Everything that Christ bought at Calvary belongs to me, and in the Name of Jesus Christ, I take what I need now!" Don't just say it under your breath. Be bold and say it out loud!

Taking Communion reminds us that we are in covenant with God and that we have certain benefits and blessings as a part of that covenant. So as you partake of the Communion emblems, say whatever it is you need in your life.

For example, say, "I thank God for what the blood and body of the Lord Jesus Christ have provided for me. I have health. I have protection. I have [name whatever you need]! And as I partake of the Communion emblems, I receive it—because God said it, I believe it, and that settles it!"

Make It Personal

In First Corinthians chapter 11, Paul told us that Jesus said He was giving His body and blood for you and me.

1 CORINTHIANS 11:23–25

23 . . . The Lord Jesus, on the night he was betrayed, took bread,

24 and when he had given thanks, he broke it and said, "This is my body, WHICH IS FOR YOU; do this in remembrance of me."

25 In the same way, after supper he took the cup, saying, "This cup is the new covenant in my blood; DO THIS, WHENEVER YOU DRINK IT, in remembrance of me."

Jesus took bread, gave thanks, broke it, and said, "This is My body which is for . . ." For *whom*? In the Bible it says, "*You.*" Jesus was speaking to His disciples, and they include you and me. So I can change the word "you" to the word "me" to make these verses more personal when I read them.

I like to read the Bible on a personal level. I apply the promises of God to my life by reading them as if they were written to me—because they were! When I read those verses of Scripture, I say, "His body was broken for *me*. His blood was shed for *me*!"

As you partake of Communion, you, too, can make it personal. You might read those verses in First Corinthians chapter 11 and think, *Oh, that's talking about the Body of Christ in general.* Yes, those verses *are* for the Body of Christ, but who is part of the Body of Christ? *You are!*

I call the Communion Table *my* table of blessing. You can call it *your* table of blessing to make it personal. When we come together as a church family and take Communion, it has significance for us as a corporate body but also for each individual believer.

In team sports, there's individual participation because each person has his or her own position to play. But there's also team participation because all the members have to work together. Well, the church is like a team. Each of us does our individual part, but we also all work together as a corporate body of believers.

I want you to understand that as we partake of the bread and the cup, we are partakers of the divine flow of blessings from the Throne of God. Communion is God's idea. It is part of His great redemptive plan. We experience God's healing power because Jesus' body was broken, and we partake of new life because Jesus hung on the Cross, shed His blood, died, and rose again. As we partake of Communion, we must release our faith and receive all that this Table provides for us.

Taking Communion Takes Faith

Jesus said, "Take, eat: this is my body. . . . This cup is the new testament in my blood: this do ye, as oft as ye drink it in remembrance of me" (1 Cor. 11:24–25 *KJV*). So how are we to partake of the body and blood of the Lord? First, we do it by faith. When we partake of Communion, we're partaking of a small amount of natural sustenance by eating the bread or wafer and drinking the cup. This act doesn't require any faith on our part. But more importantly, we're also partaking of every blessing that Jesus' death, burial, and resurrection secured for us. This act *does* require that our faith be active.

As we've said, the Communion bread and cup are symbols, or reminders. We partake of them in the natural realm to remind us of what we are doing by faith in the spiritual realm.

We take Communion the same way we got saved—*by faith*. We believe on the Lord Jesus Christ and enter into a relationship with the Heavenly Father by faith.

ROMANS 10:9–10

9 That if you confess with your mouth, "Jesus is Lord," and believe in your heart that God raised him from the dead, you will be saved.

10 For it is with your heart that you believe and are justified, and it is with your mouth that you confess and are saved.

Romans 10:9–10 says that if you believe in your heart that Jesus is Lord and you say it with your mouth, you will be saved. In the same way, when we partake of Communion we must believe that the body of the Lord Jesus Christ was broken for our healing and that His blood was shed for the remission of our sins. By faith, we believe it. Then we act on that belief by physically receiving the Communion elements. The life of the Christian is a life of faith. Partaking of Communion reminds us of what Christ did for us on the Cross, and that reminder strengthens our faith in the Lord.

Don't Partake Unworthily

When we consider how we should partake of the Communion Table, we've seen that we must be active participants, not spectators. And we've looked at the need to come to the Table by faith in order to receive through faith all of the blessings that God has provided for us through Jesus. But we must also remember that Communion is a time for us to judge ourselves. It's an occasion for us to examine ourselves, take inventory, and make changes wherever necessary. Blessings and promises accompany the Communion Table, but so does a warning. We need to be aware of the blessings *and* the warning before we partake.

1 CORINTHIANS 11:27–32

27 Therefore, whoever eats the bread or drinks the cup of the Lord in an unworthy manner will be guilty of sinning against the body and blood of the Lord.

28 A man ought to examine himself before he eats of the bread and drinks of the cup.

29 For anyone who eats and drinks without recognizing the body of the Lord eats and drinks judgment on himself.

30 That is why many among you are weak and sick, and a number of you have fallen asleep [or died].

31 But if we judged ourselves, we would not come under judgment.

32 When we are judged by the Lord, we are being disciplined so that we will not be condemned with the world.

As I mentioned in an earlier chapter, strife and division were running rampant in the church at Corinth. The believers there were not properly discerning the Lord's body. They were not treating the Lord's Supper with respect, and they were not walking in love toward one another. As a result, many of them became sick or died (1 Cor. 11:30).

First Corinthians 11:27–32 warns us to examine ourselves—our thoughts, words, and actions—before we approach the Lord's Table so that we won't have to be disciplined by God. We are to judge ourselves so that we won't be judged (v. 31).

Verse 28 tells us to examine ourselves. It doesn't tell me to examine you, or you to examine me. As we examine ourselves, if we need to make changes, we should make them. We must not allow anything to keep us from partaking of the blessings God has for us at the Communion Table!

Before we participate in the ordinance of Communion, we need to make sure that our heart is right. We must make sure that we're prepared to receive the Lord's Supper. Paul said that anyone who partakes of the Lord's Supper without recognizing the Body of Christ is inviting judgment upon himself. So before we partake of Communion, we should ask ourselves, *Am I living up to my commitment to God? Am I obeying His commandments?*

The Communion Table is a table of blessing, and there is a judgment side for those who partake of the Lord's Table in an unworthy manner. But there is a worthy way to come to the Lord's Table.

Let me explain something here. The cup reminds us that the blood of the Lord Jesus Christ has made us worthy to fellowship with God. In other words, we have been made righteous. The blood of Jesus has been applied to our hearts and has made us worthy to come into the Throne Room of God. But we must still treat Communion with reverence. We must have respect for our Heavenly Father, Jesus, and our fellow believers, and we must have regard for the significance of this holy memorial.

Communion is a solemn religious ceremony. The Lord's Supper is not a sacrifice, but a celebration which points back to the greatest sacrifice ever made—Jesus' death on the Cross that redeemed mankind from sin, sickness, poverty, and spiritual death.

1 PETER 1:18–19

18 For you know that it was not with perishable things such as silver or gold that YOU WERE REDEEMED from the empty way of life handed down to you from your forefathers,

19 but WITH THE PRECIOUS BLOOD OF CHRIST, A LAMB WITHOUT BLEMISH OR DEFECT.

For many years, the Israelites sacrificed animals to atone for, or cover over, their sin. But we were not to be redeemed with the blood of bulls or goats, or even a lamb. God's plan was that we be redeemed with the precious blood of Jesus Christ, the holy, perfect Lamb of God.

There is so much significance to the Holy Communion and yet sometimes we treat it so lightly. I pray that we will always treat Communion with reverence because it is the very essence and heart of the Gospel.

The Communion Table speaks to us as believers and calls us to come. But it calls us to be active participants, not bystanders, and to remember our vital union with Christ. It calls us to come by faith, and to accept through faith all that Jesus has provided for us. And it cautions us to examine ourselves, lest we approach the Table in an unworthy manner. *How* we partake of Communion is just as important as *why* we partake!

— CHAPTER 6 —

DO THIS IN
REMEMBRANCE OF ME

Let me go over with you again exactly what goes on in the Lord's Supper and why it is so centrally important. I received my instructions from the Master himself and passed them on to you. The Master, Jesus, on the night of his betrayal, took bread. Having given thanks, he broke it and said, This is my body, broken for you. Do this to remember me. After supper, he did the same thing with the cup: This cup is my blood, my new covenant with you. Each time you drink this cup, remember me. What you must solemnly realize is that every time you eat this bread and every time you drink this cup, you reenact in

your words and actions the death of the Master.
You will be drawn back to this meal again and
again until the Master returns. You must never
let familiarity breed contempt.

—1 Corinthians 11:23–26 (*Message*)

Have you ever spent time reminiscing about something nice that someone did for you? Did you remind yourself how great it was and how good you felt? Well, that's what we're supposed to do when we partake of Communion. We're to reminisce about the wonderful thing Jesus did for us on the Cross.

In First Corinthians 11:23–26, the Apostle Paul reminds us that we are to take the bread and the cup in remembrance of what Christ did for us on the Cross at Calvary. We're to remember the redemption that Jesus purchased for us, and the divine healing and limitless provision that He made available for us.

Every time we hold the Communion elements in our hands—the bread representing Jesus' broken body and the cup representing Jesus' shed blood—we are not only looking back at what Jesus did, but we are also looking forward to when He will come again. Jesus made it very clear that He was coming again.

JOHN 14:1–3 (*NKJV*)

1 "Let not your heart be troubled; you believe in God, believe also in Me.

2 In My Father's house are many mansions; if it were not so, I would have told you. I go to prepare a place for you.

3 And if I go and prepare a place for you, I WILL COME AGAIN AND RECEIVE YOU TO MYSELF; that where I am, there you may be also."

Almost every time Jesus talked to His disciples about His upcoming death, He reassured them that He would return. Jesus went to Heaven to prepare a place for us, and He will return. While we wait for His glorious appearing, we partake of Communion to proclaim the Lord's death until He comes again.

First Corinthians 11:26 says, *"For whenever you eat this bread and drink this cup, you proclaim the Lord's death until he comes."* The *New Century Version* says, ". . . you are telling others about the Lord's death until he comes." *The Living Bible* says, ". . . you are re-telling the message of the Lord's death, that he has died for you. Do this until he comes again." The *New Living Translation* says, ". . . you are announcing the Lord's death until he comes again." *The Amplified Bible* says, ". . . you are representing and signifying and proclaiming the fact of the Lord's death until He comes [again]."

You see, we are supposed to be proclaiming Jesus' death until He comes back. We have a job to do. When we proclaim the Lord's death, we are proclaiming the plan of salvation. It is our responsibility to proclaim the Lord's death to as many people as possible.

Now is the time for us to talk to the world about salvation, because today is the day of salvation (2 Cor. 6:2). It's up to each believer—not just the preachers, but every Christian—to tell people about Jesus. By proclaiming the Lord's death until He comes, we're telling people that Jesus died for their sins, that He rose from the grave, and that He's coming again!

Keep It Simple

The Gospel message is simple. When you tell someone about Jesus, you can either keep your message simple, or you can "fancy it up," making your message sound complex and deeply theological. But if you choose to make it complex and use difficult theological terms, most people won't understand what you're trying to say. I advise you to keep it simple.

Unfortunately, some preachers and theologians have made the Gospel complex and difficult to understand. But the Gospel is simple. We don't have to use words that only a Bible scholar would know. We can use everyday language to get the message of salvation across.

Preachers aren't the only ones who sometimes forget to speak in everyday language. The same thing can happen when you're talking to a banker about money or a mechanic about a car.

For example, my brother-in-law is a banker, and I also have a friend who's a banker. They can talk to me about finances, but if they use banking terms that only people in their industry can understand, I don't know what they're saying. I have to remind them that I'm a preacher, not a banker. Then they begin to talk in everyday language, and I understand exactly what they're saying. Really, the bankers say the same thing both times, but the words they use make the difference between my getting confused or my understanding what they're saying.

If a mechanic talked to you about your car in mechanic's terms, you might understand part of what he was saying. But if he told you the same thing in simpler terms, most likely you would understand much more of what was going on with your vehicle.

That's the way it is with Communion. People try to make it something mysterious or hard to understand, but the Communion Table is simple. It says, "Jesus died, rose, and is coming again." And that's the message we're to proclaim until Jesus returns. Let's proclaim the message of Jesus in a way that people can easily understand and accept. Let's keep it simple!

Now I want to look at some specific things we can do each day to proclaim Jesus' death until He comes. These responsibilities will keep us busy until His return.

Occupy Until He Comes

The first thing we are to do is *occupy until Jesus comes.* Jesus told a story about servants who were to occupy until their master returned. This teaching will help us see what *our* duty is.

LUKE 19:12–13 (*KJV*)

12 . . . A certain nobleman went into a far country to receive for himself a kingdom, and to return.

13 And he called his ten servants, and delivered them ten pounds, and said unto them, Occupy till I come.

The Greek word translated *occupy* carries the meaning "to trade; to do business." We see this more clearly in some modern Bible translations. Here is the *New King James*:

LUKE 19:12–13 *(NKJV)*

12 ". . . A certain nobleman went into a far country to receive for himself a kingdom and to return.

13 "So he called ten of his servants, delivered to them ten minas, and said to them, 'Do business till I come.' "

Before the nobleman left on his journey, he gave his instructions to his servants, and he left provisions to carry out those instructions. The servants were to do business for the nobleman until he returned. The servants weren't supposed to take a vacation or rest while the master was away. They were supposed to continue doing their jobs, never knowing the exact moment their master would come back.

This story is a parable. Jesus used parables to teach truths He wanted to keep hidden from unbelievers. In this parable, Jesus was telling His disciples what they were supposed to do in His absence. They were to occupy, or do business, until He returned. Jesus commanded His disciples to spread the Gospel, and we have been assigned the same task.

MATTHEW 28:18–20

18 Then Jesus came to them and said, "All authority in heaven and on earth has been given to me.

19 Therefore go and make disciples of all nations, baptizing them in the name of the Father and of the Son and of the Holy Spirit,

20 and teaching them to obey everything I have commanded you. And surely I am with you always, to the very end of the age.

What kind of business are we supposed to do until Jesus returns? We're supposed to do the Father's business. We're supposed to tell people that Jesus lived a sinless life, died on a cruel Cross, arose with victory, and is coming again! Our job is to tell others about salvation, healing, provision, safety, and deliverance until Jesus returns. And the Father has given us instructions and the provision to carry out our assignment. Jesus *is* coming back—we don't know when, but we must occupy until He comes. That means we must be about the Father's business. We are to keep doing what God has told us to do. We are to keep sharing the Gospel.

When Jesus comes back to earth, will He find us carrying out His instructions, making sure that every person on earth hears the Gospel message? Or will He find us going to church or special meetings where we clap our hands and sing and shout but do nothing once we walk out the doors?

Don't misunderstand me. There's certainly a place for church services and for special meetings full of rejoicing. Those times are good. But that is not what our business is! Our business is to go out and tell people about Jesus and lead them to salvation. That's what we're supposed to be doing until Jesus returns.

Go Into All the World
and Preach the Gospel

In the Great Commission, Jesus gave us a job to do. We have been assigned to proclaim Jesus' death until He comes by proclaiming His Gospel to the whole world.

MARK 16:15 (*KJV*)

15 And he [Jesus] said unto them, Go ye into all the world, and preach the gospel to every creature.

Many people read Mark 16:15 and think, *That's the preacher's job.* No, it's not! It's *our* job! Preaching the Gospel is *every* believer's responsibility. It's my duty to preach it from the pulpit, but it's your duty to preach it in your world. This verse is not just talking to pulpit preachers; it's talking to every member of the Body of Christ. You have the opportunity to proclaim the Gospel in places that I may never go and to people that I may never see—such as at your job with your coworkers or in your community with your neighbors.

We're all responsible for going into the world and proclaiming the Lord's death until He comes. That doesn't mean that you have to leave your job and become a missionary. "All the world" includes *your* world, not just the global world. Your world consists of your family and friends, your neighbors, the people you work with, and your community.

To whom in your world can you proclaim the death of the Lord Jesus Christ? Who can you lead to salvation? Who in your world can you pray for to be healed? Who can you lead from darkness and confusion to peace, tranquility, and joy?

Think about where you go on a regular basis. Does anyone there know you're a Christian? When you go shopping or to work, can people tell that you're a child of God? Are you proclaiming the Gospel, not just by opening your mouth and preaching all the time, but by conducting yourself in a manner that would make people say, "That's a godly person"? If someone observed you in your daily life, would he or she see Christ?

You have opportunities to proclaim the Lord's death to people in your world. You may be sitting down in a restaurant eating a hamburger when you notice that someone keeps walking by your table. That's an opportunity. That person isn't coming over and talking to you just to be talking. They've been drawn to you because they need something, and your spirit is reaching out to them saying, *I have the Answer. It's Jesus.* So start up a conversation with that person. Many times, you'll start out talking about something else, and before you know it, you'll have an opportunity to share the Gospel.

Taking Communion during a church service is not the only way to proclaim the Lord's death. We can go out into the world and preach the Gospel until He comes, proclaiming salvation through His death, burial, and resurrection.

Demonstrate Your Faith

So the first thing we do to show forth, or proclaim, the Lord's death until He comes is *to occupy.* In other words, we're to be about the Father's business until Jesus returns. The second thing we're to do is *to demonstrate faith.*

LUKE 18:8 (*NKJV*)

8 ". . . When the Son of Man comes, will He really find faith on the earth?"

Jesus expects to find faith being demonstrated on the earth when He returns. But will He? That's a question you and I have to answer. Living by faith is what we as believers are supposed to do. Unfortunately, there are many Christians who started out strong in faith but gave up somewhere along the way.

It's not how you *start* that's important. It's how you *finish!* In sports, you could score a lot of points in the first half of a game, but if you quit playing in the second half, you would lose. No matter what happens in the game of life, you have to keep living by faith. Your faith will see you through to victory!

Let me give you an example from my life of when I could have given up. I played fast-pitch softball for many years in a church league in Texas. In one game in particular, our chances of winning didn't look good. But I didn't give up or quit the game. I stayed focused on the goal of winning and did everything in my power to achieve victory.

In this particular softball game, we were tied going into the bottom of the ninth inning. Our team had to score in order to win the game. I was on first base and stole second. The next batter hit a ground ball and got thrown out at first, leaving me hung up at second.

Our team had one out. I said to myself, *I have to get over to third somehow. I have to get in a better position to score.* So I stole third base. The next guy up hit a ground ball right to the shortstop and was thrown out at first. I still couldn't go home, and now we had two outs!

I thought, *This isn't working. I have to score!* So I bluffed a steal, running down the line two or three times. The catcher would look at me, and I'd run back to third base. But the catcher got lazy. I had been watching him, and I knew it. So I started down the line again, and when he looked at me this time I acted as though I was going to turn around and run back to third base again. As soon as I saw his hand go forward to throw the ball to the pitcher, I started running as fast as I could. I stole home—and we won the game!

At the beginning of that game, it looked like we weren't going to win. I could have given up right then. But I kept doing what I knew to do, and it paid off!

Let me give you another sports example of living by faith— an illustration from car racing.

I've been interested in oval track car racing since I was a kid in school. In fact, in junior high I read every book my library had on racing, racecars, racecar drivers, and so forth. As an adult, I've also driven in a lot of races.

I know from research and experience that a driver can start out up front in a race and still not win. Every driver wants *to finish* up front. There will be things along the way that can cause problems for the drivers. If the caution flag is thrown, cars can get into a traffic jam and cause a driver to be stuck 20 cars behind the leader. That stuck driver could say, "I don't have a chance at winning. I'm just going to stay back here and finish the race."

But what good is finishing in last place? No one enters a race because he or she wants to lose. Drivers enter because they want to win and they believe they can. Drivers demonstrate their faith by *entering* the race. And they have to demonstrate their faith *to stay* in the race, maneuvering their way through traffic to get to the front. Drivers also have to demonstrate their faith *to finish* the race, especially if they want *to win*!

Now those are two natural examples, but this principle also applies to spiritual things. To be successful in life, you have to *believe* God's Word and *speak* it in faith. But you also have to *act* on the Word of God. And you have to keep believing, speaking, and acting even when the devil comes against you.

You may feel as though it's the bottom of the ninth, you're on third with two outs, and you're 60 long feet away from scoring. But you're going to have to demonstrate faith! And you may feel as though you've already lost the race, but you're going to have to keep acting on your faith.

We can choose to look around at our circumstances and just resign ourselves to accept them. But that's not what the Word tells us to do. The Word says we should use our faith until Jesus returns.

Yes, you're going to face difficulties in life. You're going to have some problems during the race, so to speak. But you've got to keep exercising your faith. You exercise your faith by staying in the race, by faithfully carrying out God's will for your life, and by keeping your eyes on Jesus all the way to the finish line.

HEBREWS 12:1–2 (*NLT*)

1 Therefore, since we are surrounded by such a huge crowd of witnesses to the life of faith, let us strip off every weight that slows us down, especially the sin that so easily hinders our progress. And let us run with endurance the race that God has set before us.

2 We do this by keeping our eyes on Jesus, on whom our faith depends from start to finish. He was willing to die a shameful death on the cross because of the joy he knew would be his afterward. Now he is seated in the place of highest honor beside God's throne in heaven.

In order to finish your race, you have to believe and speak in faith. But you also have to act. You have to do something to demonstrate your faith. And don't give up or let your faith go when obstacles block your way. Even if winning seems impossible, don't give up. Then you can say with the Apostle Paul, "But none of these things move me, neither count I my life dear unto myself, so that I might finish my course with joy, and the ministry, which I have received of the Lord Jesus, to testify the gospel of the grace of God" (Acts 20:24 *KJV*).

Remember, you cannot be defeated if you will not quit! When Jesus returns to the earth, He wants to find faith. Will He find it in you? Will you be able to say, "I have fought a good fight, I have finished my course, I have kept the faith" (2 Tim. 4:7 *KJV*)?

So by demonstrating our faith, we proclaim the Lord's death until He comes. Jesus told us to partake of the Communion Table "in remembrance of me." Participating in Communion is one way we can keep our eyes on Jesus, as Paul told us to do in Hebrews 12:2.

Don't Go to Heaven Empty-Handed

Do you know that we can use our faith for more than our own personal benefit? We can use our faith to help bring others into the Kingdom of God.

Many Christians know how to use their faith to believe God for their own personal benefit. And there's nothing wrong with believing God for His blessings in our lives. Thank God for all of our blessings. But serving God is not some kind of "Bless Me Club." We're not in this for what we can get out of it.

I encourage you to believe God for His blessings in your life. But I also encourage you to use the same faith that you believe God with for finances, houses, cars, and all other material things, and believe God to meet people whom you can lead into His kingdom.

It's sad, but many people miss out on one of life's greatest thrills. Sure, it's a thrill to take the checkered flag when you win a car race. It's a thrill to score the winning basket, run, or goal. It's a thrill to get a new house or car or even a new suit. But there is no thrill like leading someone to the Lord Jesus Christ! That's the greatest thrill of all!

When we partake of Communion in remembrance of Jesus, we can remember why He came—to seek and save those who are lost. And as we continue His ministry on the earth, we show that we *do* remember Him, and we are busy about the Father's business. When we stand before Christ, we will receive our reward for what we've done for God. If we've prayed for people, led people to the Lord, and used our faith for the sake of the Kingdom of God, we'll have given Jesus something to reward us for.

People say you can't take anything to Heaven with you. Yes, you can! You can't take material things with you to Heaven, but you can take the people for whom you exercised your faith. You can take the people you prayed with and helped bring into salvation. Yes, you *can* take something to Heaven with you— other believers. So don't go to Heaven empty-handed!

At RHEMA Bible Church we have signs over the doors leading from the auditorium to the lobby that say, "The worship is over. Now the service begins." We placed the signs there to remind us all that the auditorium is where we worship God, and the world is where we serve Him.

Communion is a very sacred and special time when we proclaim the Lord's death. It means so much to us—it touches our very core because of what God has done for us. When we partake of Communion, we thank God for salvation and healing. But is that as far as it's supposed to go? Is Communion supposed to stop with our enjoying the benefits of the Table? So many times that's where it ends. But it shouldn't!

Jesus has commissioned us to go out into the world and proclaim His death to those who are hurting and dying with no hope of eternal life. As we go about our everyday tasks—going to school or work, shopping, playing, or working out—our very life should preach the Gospel, or proclaim the Lord's death, until He comes.

Are you going to be about the Father's business? The choice is yours. You can sit back and enjoy the benefits by yourself. Or you can enjoy the benefits while proclaiming the Gospel of the Lord Jesus Christ to others so that they, too, can enjoy them. Don't allow anyone to live and die in sin, sickness, or lack, while you enjoy the benefits of the Savior. Go into your world and proclaim salvation, healing, deliverance, and prosperity to all who will receive.

We need to be more concerned about seeing people born again than we are about our own material needs. Thank God that He will provide for us. I think God told us He would meet our needs so we would focus on serving Him and not on trying to take care of ourselves. But we need a vision for the lost such as we've never had before, so that we will be about God's business and proclaim His Son's death until He comes.

As we partake of Communion, let us do so in remembrance of Jesus—in the joy of proclaiming what God has done for us, and for all mankind, through Jesus. But let us also consecrate ourselves to go out into the field and help harvest a crop of souls by letting the world know Jesus Christ is the Answer for everything they need. It's time to go forth in remembrance of Jesus and proclaim the Lord's death until He comes.

— CHAPTER 7 —

HAVE YOU READ THE WILL?

For it was from the Lord that I received the facts which, in turn, I handed on to you; how that the Lord Jesus, on the night He was to be betrayed, took some bread, and after giving thanks He broke it and said, "This is my body which is about to be broken for you. Do this in memory of me." In the same way, when the meal was over, He also took the cup. "This cup," He said, "is the new Covenant of which my blood is the pledge. Do this, every time that you drink it, in memory of me." For every time that you eat this bread and drink from the cup, you are proclaiming the Lord's death—until He returns.

—1 Corinthians 11:23–26 (*Weymouth*)

Communion is a time when we celebrate our salvation and remember the death, burial, and resurrection of Christ. Communion is also a time for us to remember the "will" of God. Just as with the written will of any other person, the will that Jesus left us went into effect after His death. Have you read the will? Referring again to our text for this book—First Corinthians 11:23–26—I want to focus on what belongs to us as heirs of God and co-heirs with Christ.

In both verses 24 and 25, Jesus said, "Do this in memory (or remembrance) of me." In these verses we're told to remember Christ's death. The question is: *Why* did Jesus tell us to remember His death? Was it for sentimental reasons? Was it for educational or historical purposes? I believe this is the reason: God wants us to know and understand what Jesus' death means to us—and Hebrews 9:15–17 makes it clear.

HEBREWS 9:15-17

15 For this reason Christ is the mediator of a new covenant, that those who are called may receive the promised eternal inheritance—now that he has died as a ransom to set them free from the sins committed under the first covenant.

16 In the case of a will, it is necessary to prove the death of the one who made it,

17 because a will is in force only when somebody has died; it never takes effect while the one who made it is living.

Through His death, Jesus Christ became the Mediator of the New Covenant. A *mediator* is "a go-between, a reconciler."

Jesus Christ is our "Go-Between." He's our Reconciler in that He reconciled us to God.

Have you ever heard or read about how something caused a rift in a family, and then a mediator had to step in? Maybe a father told his son, "I'm going to write you out of my will." Then another family member said, "Wait a minute, Dad. Come on, think about what you're saying," and repaired the relationship between the father and son. That person acted as a mediator, intervening in the situation and bringing the family back together. Therefore, when the will is read, everyone will receive an inheritance—no one will have been written out.

This scenario is similar to what Christ did for us! He is our Mediator. Our sin had separated us from God, causing a rift between us. We had been written out of the Father's will! Then Jesus intervened and reconciled us to God so that we might receive our portion of the will—the promised eternal inheritance (Heb. 9:15).

We must first realize that the *Word* of God is the *will* of God. Then we need to understand the significance of Christ's death so that we can have what the will says belongs to us.

Death Activates a Will

Jesus Christ's death put God's will into force. You see, a will does not take effect until the person who wrote it has died.

Let's read Hebrews 9:15–17 again, paying special attention to verses 16 and 17.

HEBREWS 9:15-17

15 For this reason Christ is the mediator of a new covenant, that those who are called may receive the promised eternal inheritance—now that he has died as a ransom to set them free from the sins committed under the first covenant.

16 In the case of a will, it is necessary to prove the death of the one who made it,

17 because A WILL IS IN FORCE ONLY WHEN SOMEBODY HAS DIED; it never takes effect while the one who made it is living.

God's will for us did not go into effect until Jesus died. But the will of God existed in God's mind before we ever existed. And the Holy Spirit inspired men to write down the will of God, which we call the Bible, so we would know what God's will is. The Bible is the written will of God.

Someone might ask, "Why was it necessary for God's will to be written down?" It was necessary in order to ensure that His will would be carried out! A will is a legal document that is usually written, notarized, sealed, and put away until the one who wrote it dies; and then it goes into force.

Have you ever written a will for yourself or helped someone else write theirs? If so, have you read either will lately? Probably not. It's usually not until someone dies that all the heirs gather together to read the will and discover what the deceased person wished to leave as his or her inheritance.

Your Divine Inheritance

To find out what we have received as heirs of God, we must read the will of God. The Bible tells us what we inherited.

ROMANS 8:17

17 Now if we are children, then we are heirs— heirs of God and co-heirs with Christ. . . .

GALATIANS 3:29

29 If you belong to Christ, then you are Abraham's seed, and HEIRS ACCORDING TO THE PROMISE.

We know that Jesus Christ is the Heir of God, but believers have also become heirs of God and been made joint-heirs with Jesus Christ. In other words, through accepting Christ, we become joint-heirs with Him (Rom. 8:17).

My sister and I are the only children in our family. Therefore, we are joint-heirs of our parents' estate. You might be a natural heir in *your* family. If the inheritance is not yours *yet* but will be someday, you're an *heir-apparent.* In other words, you haven't received it yet, but you know that it has been set aside for you. Or you may have already received an earthly inheritance because a will was put into effect when one of your relatives passed on.

But do you realize that you're an heir to something far greater than what your natural parents may give you? The Bible says that you are an heir of God and a joint-heir with Jesus Christ. Therefore, the promises of God's will are yours! You need to get hold of that fact. You need to know that you're not broke. You're not down and out. God's will was written to tell you about what you have as a joint-heir with Jesus Christ. That means that everything Jesus Christ inherited, you inherited too!

ROMANS 8:17 (*KJV*)

17 And if children, then heirs; heirs of God, and joint-heirs with Christ . . . .

ROMANS 8:17 (*TLB*)

17 And since we are his children we will share his treasures—for all God gives to his Son Jesus is now ours too.

God made it possible for believers to be joint-heirs with Jesus Christ. Christ's death put the will of God into effect in our lives. You see, Christ's death on the Cross was necessary so that the plan of God could be accomplished and we could become the beneficiaries of God's will.

Second Corinthians 1:20 says, "*For no matter how many promises God has made, they are 'Yes' in Christ. . . .*" Jesus' death entitled us to every promise in the will. The answer is yes! Yes, the will is in effect. Yes, we are entitled to the blessings of God. Yes, we can have salvation! Yes, we can have healing! Yes, prosperity is ours! Yes, peace and joy belong to us! We have something the world doesn't have. But they can have it too if they choose to believe on the Lord Jesus Christ and become heirs of God with us!

Christ is the Heir of God, and He has received the promises of God. He is seated at the right hand of the Father. He has received the glory He knew before He came to earth. He has been given the Name that is higher than all other names. All things have been put under His feet—He has received all authority in Heaven and in earth—and He gave that authority to us to use in His Name. As believers in Christ, we are made joint-heirs with Him, so we are also entitled to receive all that the will of God has promised!

You Can Enjoy
Your Inheritance *Now*!

Unfortunately, too many Christians don't realize that our inheritance belongs to us *now*. They say, "Well, if God wants me to have it, He will give it to me. I'll get it in due season. I'm just going to wait for that day when God provides it for me in the sweet by-and-by." And they'll be singing that same song next week, and next year. They will be in the same spot they're in because they're relegating the blessings of God to the future.

But if you are a child of God and a joint-heir with Jesus Christ, the blessings of God are yours *now*! God has already told you in His Word all that belongs to you through Christ. He has already provided it for you. So whatever it is you need, instead of saying, "I'll get it sometime," say, "I've got it now. It's mine now. I receive it now!"

You see, people who say things like, "I'll get it someday," are speaking with their head. But those who know the Word of God speak with their heart, and their confession is based on God's Word—not on what they see! *Their* words line up with *God's* Word. Their words aren't based on circumstances, what the enemy has whispered in their ear, or how much adversity they're facing!

If you listen to what the devil says or focus on your circumstances, you'll talk doubt and unbelief. But if you'll focus on the Word of God, then you'll look circumstances and adversities in the face and say, "God said it, I believe it, and that settles it! It's mine now!"

You choose which controls your life: circumstances or the Word of God. The choice is not up to God, the preacher, your spouse, your parents, or your grandparents! It's up to *you*!

All the blessings of God belong to us right now. So quit going around saying, "I lack such and such." Start saying, "I have such and such now because God has included me in His will. I'm an heir of God. I've inherited provision! I've inherited protection. I've inherited peace!" Don't say you're confused, because when there's confusion, there's no peace, and you've inherited peace. Don't say you're fearful, because God has not given you the spirit of fear, but of power, of love, and of a sound mind. God's perfect love casts out all fear (2 Tim. 1:7; 1 John 4:18).

Every time we come to the Communion Table, we remember the death of our Savior. Paul said, *"For whenever you eat this bread and drink this cup, you proclaim the Lord's death until he comes"* (1 Cor. 11:26). When we partake of Communion, we are proclaiming to the world, to the devil, and to everyone around us, "The will of God is in force because of Christ's death. I am an heir of God, and I am partaking of all the promises that God's Word says belong to me!"

You see, it's up to you. God's written will has been put into effect. But until you become a partaker through receiving Jesus as your Savior and becoming a joint-heir with Him, you won't enjoy the blessings of God.

It works the same way in the natural. A will can be read and it can say that you have X-amount of dollars in the bank, but until you do something about it, that money never does you any good. The will says the money is there and it belongs to you. But until you take the money out of the bank and use it, that money won't help you.

The Communion Table speaks of all that Jesus' death provided for the heirs of God—salvation, adoption into God's family, deliverance, restoration, healing, prosperity, protection, peace, and everything else we need. So as we come to the Table and partake of the Communion elements, let us release our faith and receive all that the will of God says is ours!

— CHAPTER 8 —

GOD HAS PREPARED A TABLE FOR YOU!

For I received from the Lord that which I also delivered to you: that the Lord Jesus on the same night in which He was betrayed took bread; and when He had given thanks, He broke it and said, "Take, eat; this is My body which is broken for you; do this in remembrance of Me." In the same manner He also took the cup after supper, saying, "This cup is the new covenant in My blood. This do, as often as you drink it, in remembrance of Me." For as often as you eat this bread and drink this cup, you proclaim the Lord's death till He comes.

—1 Corinthians 11:23–26 (*NKJV*)

In verses 24 and 25, Jesus was telling us to remember what He was about to do for us at Calvary. By calling that to mind as we partake of Communion, we can receive the reality of it in our life.

We must remember that God has prepared a Table *for us*. When people come to my house to eat and sit down at the table, I usually say, "If you don't get enough to eat, it's your own fault." I picked up that saying when I was a kid. In other words, the food is here for you to eat, so if you don't eat enough, you're the one to blame!

The same rule applies at God's Table. He has put salvation, forgiveness, restoration, safety, healing, deliverance, prosperity, and every other blessing on the Table. If you don't get enough, it's your own fault.

The Table is already prepared. Christ began to prepare the Table when He said, "It is finished," the breath escaped His lungs, and His head slumped to His chest. Then through His burial and resurrection, Jesus set the Table with everything we need.

As a Christian, you can come to this Table anytime. What's on the Table belongs to you, and you belong at the Table. God prepared the Table with you in mind. So come to the Table!

Have you ever been watching television or doing something else before a meal was ready and then heard the cook say, "Come and eat—the food is on the table"? Around my house, when my wife, Lynette, says it's time to come and eat, you'd better get there because she doesn't like people to eat cold food!

Well, God has prepared a Table for us. It was paid for by the blood of the Lord Jesus Christ. Everything we need is on this Table, and it all belongs to us. God *has prepared* the Table. He's not *going to* prepare it. It's ready now! The bread and the cup represent all the blessings of God that Jesus provided for us.

You Have a Reservation

I want you to understand that if you know Jesus Christ as your personal Savior, you belong at the Lord's Table. You have a reservation. There's a place at the Table with your name on it! Let's say you go to a banquet and the hostess says, "You're sitting at table number 5." You walk around the banquet hall, find table 5, and look at the place cards until you find your name. That's *your* seat. It's reserved for *you*.

God prepared a place for you at the Table when Jesus died on the Cross, and He put your name on it! Nobody else can sit in your chair. You don't have to push your way in. You don't have to ask someone to get out of your seat. That is *your* chair. That's *your* place—and yours alone!

PSALM 23:5 (*KJV*)

5 Thou preparest a table before me in the presence of mine enemies: thou anointest my head with oil; my cup runneth over.

This verse says that God prepares a table for us in the presence of our enemies. That means the door is open and the table is prepared, but there will be some adversaries standing around watching. Whether or not you go to the table and receive what God has for you, the adversaries will still be there, so you might as well sit down and enjoy the things of God!

You can sit down at the Communion Table knowing that no weapon formed against you will prosper (Isa. 54:17). It doesn't matter what *surrounds* you. It's what is on the *inside* of you that determines your outcome and brings you into victory. And what's inside you? The Greater One lives in you!

1 JOHN 4:4 (*KJV*)

4 Ye are of God, little children, and have overcome them: because greater is he that is in you, than he that is in the world.

We have been born again, and God has poured out His Spirit on us (Acts 2:16–17). We are filled with God's Presence and full of His grace and power. And we can do all things through Christ Who strengthens us (Phil. 4:13)!

When we look at God's blessings on the Table, our adversary, Satan, likes to tell us, "You can't have them. They're not yours." But God has prepared a Table for us right in Satan's presence, and Satan can't do anything about it!

Come and Dine!

God's Table is ready for you. You don't have to wait until everything in your life is perfect before you can enjoy it. You can receive from God in spite of your circumstances. Sit down at the Table and receive what you need today, and don't worry about stocking up for the future because you can go back to the Table again tomorrow!

When I went to Bible college, I used to take a few of my buddies home with me almost every weekend. Sometimes my grandma was also visiting, and she would fix us something to eat. But most of the time, we went over to my cousins' house.

When we got there, my friends and I ate as much as we could because we knew we had to go back to eating in the college cafeteria the next day. The food at that cafeteria was not as good as it was at home!

In those days, I was as tall as I am now, which is over 6 feet, but I only weighed about 150 pounds. People joked that my legs were hollow because of how much I could eat! And I ate fast! My friends would say, "We'd better eat or Hagin will eat it for us!" I was usually already on my second helping by the time they got their first one. We all ate a lot, because we knew it would be at least another week before we had a good meal like that again.

I want you to know that when you go to God's Table, you don't have to stock up. You can come back for more later. In fact, if you want to, you can come to the Table two, three, or four times a day. And the next day you can come again! You can come to the Table any time you want to!

God has prepared a Table for you with everything you need on it. But *you* have to come to the Table. God won't bring it to you. You have to come and get it.

Out on my grandparents' farm, they used to ring the dinner bell when the food was ready. They didn't bring any food out to the field. You had to come to the house where it was waiting. Boy, when they rang that dinner bell, the farm hands came running from all over the place!

Friend, the dinner bell is ringing and there's a place set for you! Come to the Table! Come and enjoy what God has prepared for you. The Father is saying, "Pull up a chair and sit down." As the old hymn says, "Jesus has a Table spread where the saints of God are fed. He invites His chosen people, 'Come and dine.' . . . 'Come and dine,' the Master calleth, 'Come and dine;' You may feast at Jesus' table all the time; He Who fed the multitude, turned the water into wine, To the hungry calleth now, 'Come and dine.' "[1]

Whatever you need is on the Table! Jesus came that we might have life and have it more abundantly (John 10:10). *Abundantly* means there's plenty on the Table. God never runs out of His supply. There has never been a panic in Heaven because there was a shortage of blessings. If the serving dish gets a little low, they just bring out another one.

Think of going to one of those all-you-can-eat buffets. When a pan starts getting low on food, they just lift it out and put in a full one. There is always plenty to go around, and no one ever has to go home hungry.

It's similar with God's Table. God has plenty of *everything* you need. Psalm 23:5 says that our cup is running over. It's one of those bottomless cups like some restaurants have. It never runs dry!

When you come to the Communion Table, pull out your chair, sit down, pick up your plate, and start filling it with whatever you need. Take a big helping of healing and prosperity. Take a drink of the Living Water. For dessert, take a big helping of joy! Then rejoice as the devil looks on—because he can't do anything about it! You belong there!

When you partake of Communion, remember that everything you could ever need or want is on the Table. Jesus Christ purchased it with His body and blood. It's yours to enjoy today. God has prepared the Table for you! Come and dine!

---

[1] Charles B. Widmeyer, "Come and Dine."

— Chapter 9 —

The Table That Speaks

I passed on to you what I received from the Lord himself, namely, that on the night he was betrayed the Lord Jesus took a loaf, and after thanking God he broke it, saying, 'This means my body broken for you; do this in memory of me.' In the same way he took the cup after supper, saying, 'This cup means the new covenant ratified by my blood; as often as you drink it, do it in memory of me.' For as often as you eat this loaf and drink this cup, you proclaim the Lord's death until he comes.

—1 Corinthians 11:23–26 (*Moffatt*)

The Communion Table has a significance that is worth noting. I've said many times that this Table preaches the Gospel of the Lord Jesus Christ without saying a word. This Table delivers distinct messages about Jesus—*who He is to us, what He did for us,* and *His message of the Gospel.* As we look at these messages the Communion Table conveys, you will notice that they overlap and intertwine because they are so closely related.

When I read First Corinthians 11:23–26, it speaks to me of God's great plan of redemption, the plan of salvation. That plan encompasses Jesus' death, burial, resurrection, and soon-coming return. But the redemption plan began with Jesus' *life.*

The Communion Table Speaks of Jesus' Life

We know that Jesus was born in Bethlehem, wrapped in swaddling clothes, and laid in a manger. He was dedicated to God in the Temple in accordance with Jewish Law. But all that the Bible says about Jesus' boyhood is that *"Jesus grew in wisdom and stature, and in favor with God and men"* (Luke 2:52).

The next we read of Jesus, He is a young man teaching in the Temple at the age of 12. Then little else is written about Jesus until He was baptized by John. Immediately after His baptism, Jesus began His public ministry.

The Bible clearly tells us what Jesus' ministry entailed. Two passages that do so are Acts 10:38 and First John 3:8.

ACTS 10:38

38 How God anointed Jesus of Nazareth with the Holy Spirit and power, and how he went around doing good and healing all who were under the power of the devil, because God was with him.

1 JOHN 3:8 (*KJV*)

8 He that committeth sin is of the devil; for the devil sinneth from the beginning. For this purpose the Son of God was manifested, that he might destroy the works of the devil.

Jesus came to earth to destroy the works of the devil, and through teaching, preaching, healing, and performing miracles, Jesus destroyed the devil's kingdom and began to usher in the Kingdom of God!

First Corinthians 11:26 tells us to partake of Communion in remembrance of Jesus, and since Jesus instituted Communion on the night before He died, we automatically think about His agony and Crucifixion—and we should. But we also need to remember and celebrate what Jesus did for us in the years leading up to the Cross. Communion is also a remembrance of Jesus' life—and what a life! No one has blessed humanity more than He did, and does. The Apostle John said it best:

JOHN 21:25 (*KJV*)

25 And there are also many other things which Jesus did, the which, if they should be written every one, I suppose that even the world itself could not contain the books that should be written.

JOHN 20:31 (*KJV*)

31 But these are written, that ye might believe that Jesus is the Christ, the Son of God; and that believing ye might have life through his name.

Jesus did so much for mankind, that if everything were written down, the record would fill more books than the world could contain. But the things that *are* recorded in the Bible were written so that we would believe that Jesus is the Son of God and thereby receive salvation and eternal life through Him.

The Communion Table speaks of Jesus' life and the wonderful things He did before He went to the Cross, but it also speaks of what He wrought for us through His death.

The Communion Table Speaks of Jesus' Death

The Bible doesn't tell us everything that Jesus did while He was alive, but it does tell us about His death and what it means to us.

Jesus was not afraid to die. He actually looked forward to His death. But man seems to do just the opposite. Throughout the history of the world, mankind has looked for different ways to prolong life on this earth and achieve immortality.

Ponce de Leon came to America in 1513 looking for the "fountain of youth." And the search for eternal youth still goes on today. I read in the newspaper that sometime in 2005 scientists in Masada, near the Dead Sea, had found some 2,000-year-old seeds of a date palm tree. They revived those seeds and grew a plant that they nicknamed "Methuselah."

Those scientists began testing and analyzing the DNA of the plant leaves in hopes that they would find a substance or a medicine that could help people live longer and maybe even attain eternal life. What the world doesn't understand is that the only way to attain eternal life is to accept Jesus Christ as personal Savior. He is the Seed that was planted so that man could have eternal life.

Christ the Incorruptible Seed

Jesus told His disciples, "The hour has come that the Son of Man should be glorified. Most assuredly, I say to you, unless a grain of wheat falls into the ground and dies, it remains alone; but if it dies, it produces much grain" (John 12:23–24 *NKJV*). When Christ referred to a grain of wheat, He was talking about Himself. He was that Seed, and unless He was planted—unless He died—He could not be raised again and give life.

A seed dies when it is put in the ground, but out of that dead seed life rises. Jesus Christ died on the Cross. He was put in a grave. But He rose up out of the grave with new life! We can say then that Christ is the Incorruptible Seed.

Jesus also called the Word of God a seed (Luke 8:11). And John 1:14 tells us that "the Word was made flesh, and dwelt among us . . ." (*KJV*). Jesus is the *Living* Word and the Bible is the *written* Word. Both the Living Word *and* the written Word are incorruptible!

Jesus is the Incorruptible Seed. The Incorruptible Seed could not be corrupted or become infected with sin. You see, man can be corrupted, but the Son of Man could not be corrupted. Jesus knew no sin! He did not sin, but He *became* sin so that you and I could be free from sin (2 Cor. 5:21). That freedom is what the Communion Table represents.

Jesus Christ is the same yesterday, today and forever (Heb. 13:8). The Son of God suffered, bled, and died upon the Cross that you and I might live free today and enjoy life—spiritual life and also our natural life.

The Seed that I'm talking about did not come from anything on earth. It came from Heaven. God sent His Son Jesus Christ, the Incorruptible Seed, to be implanted into humanity so that we could walk from the dregs of sin to the glories of Heaven. This Seed is not natural; it's divine. This Seed is immortal and everlasting. Christ, the Incorruptible Seed, died and was placed in the ground. But His tomb is empty! Death and the grave could not hold Him because Jesus *is* life. And because the Incorruptible Seed was planted, every man, woman, boy, and girl can now receive eternal life in Heaven and abundant life on earth!

The Incorruptible Word of God

Let's look at First Peter 1:23, focusing on the last part of the verse.

1 PETER 1:23 (*NKJV*)

23 [You] having been born again, not of corruptible seed but incorruptible, through THE WORD OF GOD which LIVES AND ABIDES FOREVER.

The Word of God will live and abide forever—not for a little while or just long enough to get us by. You see, the Incorruptible Seed *Jesus Christ* gave us life and that more abundantly (John 10:10). But we access that life today by acting on the Incorruptible

Word of God. Thank God for both Incorruptible Seeds—the Living Word and the written Word!

If you're born again, you're not just a mere mortal searching for immortality and eternal life. You have it! Quit searching! We are full of resurrection power.

ROMANS 8:11 (*KJV*)

11 But if the Spirit of him that raised up Jesus from the dead dwell in you, he that raised up Christ from the dead shall also quicken your mortal bodies by his Spirit that dwelleth in you.

The same Holy Spirit Who raised Christ from the dead will quicken your mortal body. Some people say that the life of God only quickens us spiritually. But this verse says that God will quicken our *mortal body*!

Quit talking about being tired, and start talking how the power of God is quickening your mortal body. Start saying what the Word says. Start speaking in faith.

MARK 11:23 (*KJV*)

23 For verily I say unto you, That whosoever shall say unto this mountain, Be thou removed, and be thou cast into the sea; and shall not doubt in his heart, but shall believe that those things which he saith shall come to pass; he shall have whatsoever he saith.

Have you been speaking to the mountains in your life? You have the Incorruptible Seed Christ Jesus living on the inside of you. And when you learn how to speak out the Incorruptible

Word of God, believing that what you say will come to pass, it will be like a two-edged sword that cuts asunder everything that comes against you to hinder you from having abundant life!

You can rightfully say, "I have no more need, because the Incorruptible Seed has met my need." Sometimes we do too much talking about the need and not enough about the Seed. But in Mark 11:23, Jesus told us that when we believe in our hearts and speak in faith, even mountains have to move out of our way!

We believers are the most privileged people in the world. We have the Incorruptible Seed living in us, and we have the incorruptible Word of God working for us. So we can boldly say, "I am who God says I am. I have what God says I have. I can do what God says I can do!" Is it because we're something in and of ourselves? No, it's because of Jesus Christ and what He did for us!

Again, we partake of Communion to remind us of what Jesus did for us. Twice in First Corinthians 11:24–25 Jesus used the phrase "Do this in remembrance of Me." Jesus is the One Who said that we are to remember Him. We should never forget what Jesus did for us in His great redemptive work!

If we're facing trouble, disaster, or despair, we should remember Jesus because He is our Deliverer. If we're sick, we should remember Jesus because He is our Healer. If we're in need, we should remember Jesus because He is our Provider. If we're full of care, worried, or burdened, we should remember Jesus because He is our Peace. If we're healthy and prosperous and everything is going great, we should remember Jesus because He is our Good Shepherd. We should remember that all the blessings of God belong to us because of Jesus.

Count Your Blessings

As Christians we sometimes sing, "Count your blessings, Name them one by one . . . ."[1] But it would be impossible to name all of the things that God has done for us. We couldn't remember every blessing we've received from God through the years. Usually, we can only remember a few of them, and most of the ones we remember happened recently. But when we come together to commemorate our Savior's death on the Cross, we are, in effect, thanking God for every blessing He has bestowed upon us.

When we take Communion, we thank God for His great plan of redemption. That plan was made possible because of God's great love for us (John 3:16). Communion is a powerful reminder of God's love. God loved us so much that He sent His only Son to redeem us, and Jesus loved us so much that He willingly died in our place.

Jesus Became Our Substitute

Jesus instructed us to remember what He did for us. He wanted us to remember that He suffered the stripes on His back for our healing, and He took our pain and suffering so we could have His peace. He wanted us to remember that He took our poverty and lack so that we could have His abundant provision. Jesus took our sins upon Himself and bore our punishment. We need to remember all that Jesus did at Calvary, but the most important thing to remember is that *He did it for us.*

ROMANS 4:25

25 [Jesus] was delivered over to death for our sins and was raised to life for our justification.

ROMANS 8:32

32 He who did not spare his own Son, but gave him up for us all—how will he not also, along with him, graciously give us all things?

2 CORINTHIANS 5:21

21 God made him who had no sin to be sin for us, so that in him we might become the righteousness of God.

GALATIANS 3:13

13 Christ redeemed us from the curse of the law by becoming a curse for us, for it is written: "Cursed is everyone who is hung on a tree."

All of these verses say that what Jesus did, He did *for us*! Jesus took our place. Jesus became a Substitute for you and for me. A substitute is someone who takes your place when you can't be there or when you can't perform the task required.

In the game of basketball, especially toward the end of the game, if the team is behind by several points, the coach will sometimes substitute a player who can score a lot of points quickly, like a good three-point shooter. The coach puts the substitute in because he can do something that the other players can't do.

I want you to understand that Jesus Christ became our Substitute! We needed a Substitute because we could not perform the required task. We could not help ourselves. We could not extract ourselves from our sin, sickness, and lack. Jesus became our Substitute and did what we could not do. He accomplished what we could not accomplish. And He was the only One Who could be our Substitute and deliver us.

The Scriptures say, "For all have sinned, and come short of the glory of God" (Rom. 3:23 *KJV*). Jesus died on the Cross for all mankind. He died because we *all* have sinned and we all needed a Savior.

Most Christians know that John 3:16 says, *"For GOD so loved the world that he gave his one and only Son, that whoever believes in him shall not perish but have eternal life."* But we must also realize that *Jesus* loved us so much that He freely gave Himself on the Cross. God loved us and gave Jesus. Jesus loved us and gave Himself. The love that was displayed in the death of Christ accomplished what nothing else could. The God-kind of love became the solution for all of our problems.

Jesus paid for it all at Calvary. I remember the chorus of a hymn we used to sing that describes it perfectly: "Jesus paid it all, All to Him I owe; Sin had left a crimson stain, He washed it white as snow."[2]

'Paid in Full!'

Jesus, our Substitute, did something that we could not do ourselves. We owed a debt we could not pay, and Jesus paid a debt He did not owe.

I read a news story once that was entitled, "Paid in Full Program Shows God's Grace." The article said that a group of pastors in Boise, Idaho, came up with a novel way to preach the Gospel. They offered to pay people's parking tickets as a way to demonstrate God's grace. The project was called "The Grace Gift, Paid in Full."

Many people in town thought it was too good to be true. But the pastors sat at tables outside Boise City Hall for three hours with their checkbooks, ready to pay off parking tickets for Boise's residents. All the people had to do was ask.

A young man said, "A friend sent me an e-mail about it. And when I came down here and saw the sign I thought, *This is not an Internet hoax!* So I got out of my car and pulled out my seven parking tickets totaling $182 and got them all paid by the grace of God in the churches."

One young woman who had 14 parking tickets only wanted the churches to pay half because she felt so bad. But just as God's grace covered *all* our sin, the pastors covered all her debt.

Altogether, about $7,500 in parking tickets was paid in full by 70 churches from different Christian denominations working together on the project.

That was an earthly demonstration of what Christ did for us at Calvary. Jesus paid it all. Jesus became human so that we could receive the divine nature of God. He penetrated the darkness so we could walk in the light. He became sin so we could become the righteousness of God. Jesus was wounded so we could be healed. And He was taken captive so we could go free.

Have you ever received an invoice from a company? The truth is, we were sent an invoice from God.

ROMANS 6:23

23 For the wages of sin is death, but the gift of God is eternal life in Christ Jesus our Lord.

We owed a debt to God that we couldn't pay, but Jesus Christ died on the Cross and paid it all. Our invoice for salvation, redemption, baptism in the Holy Spirit, freedom from all sickness and disease, unlimited provision from God's storehouse, wisdom and understanding from the Holy Ghost, peace, and protection is now stamped "paid in full!"

We could not pay the price to extract ourselves from sin, sickness, poverty, and bondage to Satan. But Jesus Christ paid the price for us, and by faith we receive what Christ has already purchased for us.

Have you ever received an invoice stamped "paid in full"? Wasn't that exciting? Friend, when you accepted Jesus Christ as your personal Savior, the blood of the Lord Jesus Christ cleansed your heart and stamped your debt for sin "paid in full." Every blessing of salvation became yours!

The Communion Table reminds us that everything Jesus purchased on Calvary is ours. We partake of Communion to remind ourselves that our redemption and every blessing that's associated with it centers on what Jesus did at Calvary.

---

[1] Johnson Oatman, Jr. and Edwin O. Excell, "Count Your Blessings."

[2] Elvina M. Hall and John T. Grape, "Jesus Paid It All."

— CHAPTER 10 —

JESUS IS OUR CORNERSTONE

For I passed on to you the account, which I myself received from the Lord; how the Lord Jesus, on the very night he was betrayed, took bread, and when he had given thanks, he broke it, saying, "This is my body, broken for you; this do in memory of me." In the same way also, he took the cup after supper, saying: "This cup is the new covenant in my blood; do this, whenever you drink it, in memory of me." For as often as you eat this bread and drink this cup, you are proclaiming your Lord's death until he come.

—1 Corinthians 11:23–26 (*Montgomery*)

The Communion Table speaks to us of the very heart of our faith. And one message it presents to us is that Jesus is the

Cornerstone for everything we have as believers. The Cross of Christ is the foundation of our faith.

PSALM 118:22–24 (*NKJV*)

22 The stone which the builders rejected has become the chief cornerstone.

23 This was the Lord's doing; it is marvelous in our eyes.

24 This is the day the Lord has made; we will rejoice and be glad in it.

These verses are prophetic. They were written a few hundred years before Christ ever went to the Cross, but they reveal what He would do and become. Jesus was the Stone the psalmist was referring to.

Have you ever seen a cornerstone? *Webster's New World Dictionary* defines a *cornerstone* as "a stone that forms part of the corner of a building, especially a foundation stone . . . often inscribed, laid at a ceremony that marks the beginning of building; the basic, essential, or most important part; foundation."[1]

A cornerstone marks the origin of something, usually a building. But we also refer to other "cornerstones." The cornerstone of our society is the family unit. The cornerstone of our nation is the Constitution of the United States of America. And the cornerstone of our Christian life is the Bible.

A cornerstone is the foundation upon which everything else rests. It is the fundamental building block—the standard. In a building, a cornerstone designates the direction of the walls. Jesus is our Cornerstone. He sets the direction of our life.

Jesus was rejected by the religious leaders of His day. They had the Temple, the Mosaic Law, and the words of the prophets as their cornerstones. Judaism was built upon those foundations.

Jesus didn't fit in with their idea of a proper foundation. He was not the kind of Rock they wanted. He didn't set a direction they wanted to go in. So they rejected Him, His teachings, and everything He represented.

The psalmist prophesied that the people would reject Jesus as the Cornerstone, and they did. People are still rejecting Him. But everyone who accepts Him and allows Him to become their Chief Cornerstone receives abundant life!

When we take Communion, the Table speaks to us of the foundation on which it rests—Jesus. He is our Foundation and our Standard. He sets the direction in which we are to go. He became our Cornerstone through His death on Calvary, a death which gave us salvation and every blessing we have.

This Is the Day

The Communion Table also speaks to us of the dawning of a new day.

PSALM 118:24

2 This is the day the Lord has made; we will rejoice and be glad in it.

The psalmist prophesied, "*This* is the day the Lord hath made . . ." because when Jesus died on the Cross and rose again, it was the beginning of a new day. It wasn't the start of a new

24-hour day, but of a new age, a new period of time. And we are living in that same "new day."

The time period the psalmist was talking about began when the Cornerstone was laid at the Cross of Calvary. That was the beginning of *the day*. And we're still living in that day because the building, the Church, for whom the Cornerstone was laid is still being built. And the building will not be complete until Jesus comes back to receive the Church.

In the natural, when a construction crew starts a new building they first lay a cornerstone. They start at the cornerstone and build the walls, working their way around until they come back to the cornerstone. Spiritually speaking, the Church of the Lord Jesus Christ is "under construction" until Jesus, the Chief Cornerstone, comes back. That's when the last stone will be laid. Construction of the Church began with the Cornerstone, and it will end with Him.

One solemn day more than 2,000 years ago, Jesus died on a Cross. On that day, He purchased our salvation, deliverance, healing, safety, and provision. And that day is still in existence right now. The Bible calls it the day of salvation (2 Cor. 6:2). But it's no longer a day of sorrow—it's a day of great rejoicing!

Each day of our week consists of 24 hours made up of seconds and minutes. The day of salvation isn't marked by seconds, minutes, and hours the way our natural days are, but it *does* have a beginning and an end. It began when Jesus died on the Cross, and the end has not yet come. The Bible says, "No man or angel knows the day and hour when the Son of Man will come. Only the Father knows" (Matt. 24:36). God could look

over at Jesus right now and say, "Son, go bring them home" and
the "building" would be finished.

The Bible tells us that Jesus is coming back. In Acts 1:11, after
Jesus ascended to Heaven, an angel said, ". . . *This same Jesus,
who has been taken from you into heaven, will come back in the
same way you have seen him go into heaven.*" We don't know
when Jesus will return, but we don't need to focus on that. We
need to focus on doing what the Bible says to do—occupying
until He comes and proclaiming the Gospel to the world.

We must learn to face each 24-hour day in light of the day
of salvation in which the Cornerstone was laid. When we
face problems we need to say, "We are still in the day when
Jesus purchased salvation, deliverance, healing, safety, and
provision." The Cornerstone represents all those blessings and
more. So when we face sickness and pain we can look to the
Cornerstone and be healed because we are still in *that day.*
Therefore, healing and all that the Cornerstone stands for
belong to us today!

Because of that day at Calvary, we can expect certain things.
But they won't just happen for us automatically. We have to
use our faith and appropriate everything that belongs to us
according to the Word of God. We're living in a day of salvation
and deliverance—a day of victory and overcoming, health and
healing, power and strength, prosperity and blessing. This is
our time!

I read Psalm 118:24 this way: "This is the day which the
Lord hath made; *I* will rejoice and be glad in it." I make it a
confession, and it's one we all need to make every day. I confess

this verse because I'm going to enjoy this day of salvation. This is the day—the age or time period—that the Lord has made. I choose to rejoice and be glad in it—not sad, but *glad*! I'm not going to spend my time being upset about or afraid of what might happen next. I know what's going to happen next. The Bible already told me! According to the Word of God, I have safety, provision, and everything else I need for the future.

You don't have to be afraid any longer. Peace is yours when you understand the age in which you're living—and that in this age the Cornerstone has given you all the provision and protection you will ever need.

ISAIAH 49:8 (*KJV*)

8 Thus saith the Lord, In an acceptable time have I heard thee, and in a day of salvation have I helped thee: and I will preserve thee. . . .

According to this verse, God is your Helper. He will protect you, care for you, and preserve you. You might say, "But things are looking really bad." Do you remember how well God cared for the Israelites while they marched around the desert for 40 years? He provided water for them when they were thirsty. He sent them manna and quail when they got hungry. He gave them victory when they faced armies much bigger and stronger than they were. Even after the Israelites entered the Promised Land, they still faced all kinds of adversity. But every time, against all odds, they always came out on top because of what God did for them.

The same God Who took care of the children of Israel back then is taking care of *you* today. You are a child of God! Your Heavenly Father is the same God Who laid the Cornerstone. And that Cornerstone is still in place. So don't go around wondering, *What am I going to do?* Instead, say, "I have a firm foundation because of Jesus, the Cornerstone that was laid. I know God will take care of me!" Believe it, confess it, and rejoice about it!

Some people think they don't have anything to rejoice about. Well, they must not have read the Bible, because the Bible gives us plenty to rejoice about! And the Bible *tells* us to rejoice: *"Rejoice in the Lord always. I will say it again: Rejoice!"* (Phil. 4:4).

As we partake of Communion, the Table reminds us that today is the day of salvation. And salvation not only means redemption from sin and entrance into eternal life, but it also includes deliverance, healing, safety, provision, and every blessing of God. Salvation is an all-inclusive term. All that is yours through salvation is ample cause to rejoice! You have been blessed beyond measure!

Salvation wasn't available until after Jesus died, so this is the greatest time to be alive. Let us rejoice and be glad because *this* is our time. This is our day. This is when we're to enjoy life and the things of God and tell other people about the Cornerstone.

So many people are wishing and hoping that *someday* they'll be blessed. Many Christians say, "Well, everything will be all right when I get to Heaven." No! We're blessed now! According to the Word of God, everything is all right *now*. We can receive what we need from God *today*. This is our day! Let's rejoice and be glad in it!

It's okay to look to the future and set goals, but as you're reaching for the *possibilities of tomorrow*, don't forget to enjoy the *realities of today*. You don't have to wait for tomorrow to be happy or blessed. In reality, "tomorrow" never comes. When your "tomorrow" finally arrives, it, too, will be "today."

So just live in today. All the blessings of God are ours today because we have made Jesus our Cornerstone!

A Life *and* Death Situation

The Communion Table speaks to us of Jesus' death. The religious leaders of His day rejected Him as a mason constructing a building rejects a stone as unfit. But the Table reminds us that Jesus has become the Cornerstone of the Church—this great building of which we are all a part.

Although the Communion Table portrays death, it also stands for life. It is sort of a paradox when you think about it—we celebrate Jesus' *death* because it gave us *life*. Think about it this way: The whole purpose of Jesus' *life* was *to die* to give us *life*.

Jesus died on the Cross for all mankind so we could walk free from sin and have everlasting, abundant life. Now we have to exercise our will and choose whether we will enjoy that eternal life of blessing or suffer eternal death and damnation. We must choose whether we will enjoy Heaven or endure hell.

Many people today do not like it when preachers mention the word "hell," but there *is* a Heaven to gain and a hell to shun! Each person has to make a choice between the two.

The Communion Table represents life—life that you would not have, spiritually or physically, if it were not for the bread and the cup. This Table represents the Resurrection of the Lord Jesus Christ, who was dead but arose. It also represents *your* resurrection, because you were dead in sin but have now been raised to new life through the blood of Jesus.

EPHESIANS 2:1–5

1 As for you, YOU WERE DEAD IN YOUR TRANSGRESSIONS AND SINS,

2 in which you used to live when you followed the ways of this world and of the ruler of the kingdom of the air, the spirit who is now at work in those who are disobedient.

3 All of us also lived among them at one time, gratifying the cravings of our sinful nature and following its desires and thoughts. Like the rest we were by nature objects of wrath.

4 But because of his great love for us, GOD, WHO IS RICH IN MERCY,

5 MADE US ALIVE WITH CHRIST EVEN WHEN WE WERE DEAD IN TRANSGRES-SIONS—it is by grace you have been saved.

You were dead in your sin, but you have been raised to new life through the blood of Jesus. This resurrection is signified by water baptism. During baptism, you are submersed under the water (this is symbolic of being "buried") and then raised up again (symbolic of being "raised from the dead").

As I mentioned previously, the two ordinances of the Church are water baptism and Communion. Although water baptism does not save us, it is a picture of what happens when we enter into relationship with Christ. When we accept Jesus as our Savior, we die to sin and are raised to life with Him through the New Birth experience. Because Jesus lives, we live (Rom. 6:4–11).

Communion Is the Gospel in Its Simplest Form

Performing the Communion service is one of the most enjoyable things I do as a pastor. I thank God for the foot-stomping, hand-clapping, shouting, and laughing services that we have. I believe in those, and I enjoy those times. But I have come to enjoy the Lord's Supper more than any other service. I have come to enjoy preaching and teaching about the Lord's Table as much as I enjoy preaching about anything else. The reason is simple: the Communion Table is the Gospel in its simplest form.

I like to preach about Communion because the whole story of the Gospel is wrapped up in it. When I look at the Communion Table and see the bread and the cup I think, *That's the whole Gospel right there on the Table.* Without saying a word, the Communion emblems tell the Gospel story.

The Gospel is summed up in the death, burial, resurrection, and soon return of Jesus Christ. These are the very things the Holy Communion represents and signifies. You cannot understand Communion until you understand the Cross. You cannot understand Communion until you understand that because of the stripes that Jesus took on His body, we have physical health and healing. You cannot understand Communion until you understand that Jesus' blood washed away our sins.

Every time we eat the bread, our actions proclaim to the devil and all of his demons, "Jesus healed our bodies and made us whole!" Every time we drink of the cup, we shout victoriously, "Jesus saved us from sin!" Every time we partake of Communion, we tell the world that Jesus is coming again!

Communion tells the Gospel message in its simplest form. Here are just a few scriptures that portray the Gospel message— the Good News Jesus came to share with the world.

JOHN 3:16–17

16 "For God so loved the world that he gave his one and only Son, that whoever believes in him shall not perish but have eternal life.

17 For God did not send his Son into the world to condemn the world, but to save the world through him."

Communion is the Gospel of salvation. Jesus' precious blood was shed for our salvation (Matt. 26:28), and when we receive Jesus Christ as our personal Savior, we receive eternal life and become a part of the family of God.

1 PETER 2:24 (*KJV*)

24 Who his own self bare our sins in his own body on the tree, that we, being dead to sins, should live unto righteousness: by whose stripes ye were healed.

Communion is the Gospel of healing. When we receive Jesus as our Savior, we also receive Him as our Healer, because we were healed by the stripes He took on His body.

PSALM 23:1

1 The Lord is my shepherd, I shall not be in want.

PHILIPPIANS 4:19

19 And my God will meet all your needs according to his glorious riches in Christ Jesus.

Communion is the Gospel of prosperity. Jesus said He came to give us an abundant life (John 10:10). An abundant life is one where our needs are met and we lack nothing. When we come into the family of God, not only are our *needs* met, but our *desires* are also fulfilled (Ps. 37:4).

JOHN 14:2–3 (*NKJV*)

2 . . . I go to prepare a place for you.

3 And if I go and prepare a place for you, I will come again and receive you to Myself; that where I am, there you may be also."

ACTS 1:11

11 ". . . This same Jesus, who has been taken from you into heaven, will come back in the same way you have seen him go into heaven."

Jesus will return. Jesus went back to Heaven to prepare a place for us (John 14:2–3). He's getting everything ready for the day when God says, "Son, go get My children." Then Jesus will descend from Heaven on the clouds with power and great glory and take us home (see Matt. 24:30; 1 Thess. 4:16–17; Rev. 1:7).

That is the Gospel message—salvation, healing, prosperity, and the soon return of the Lord Jesus Christ. Thank God for all of the benefits we have, and for Communion which represents each and every one. "Bless the Lord, O my soul, and forget not all his benefits" (Ps. 103:2 *KJV*)!

The benefits of the Kingdom of God become yours when you receive Jesus and His Gospel. God bestows His benefits on His family, and when you accept Jesus as your Savior, you become a child of God!

In the natural, there are benefits that belong to employees simply because they work for a particular company. But those "*employee* benefits" aren't for just anyone. True, the benefits always exist, but they can only be yours if you become an employee.

In a similar way, if you haven't been born again, the Kingdom benefits don't belong to you. But when you accept Jesus Christ as your Savior, the blessings and benefits of God are yours! (If you have never accepted Jesus as your Savior and you want to do so, please turn to the prayer at the back of this book.)

The Communion Table still speaks to us today every time we approach it. That Table tells us that Jesus—the Cornerstone of our faith—shed His blood to redeem us from sin and cleanse us of all unrighteousness. The Table declares to us that Jesus allowed His body to be broken to free us from sickness and disease. The Table reminds us that God has provided abundantly for us. And the Table announces to us that the Lord will soon return! The Communion Table still speaks to us today. As we heed its message, our lives will be blessed!

---

[1] David B. Guralnik, ed., Webster's New World Dictionary, 2nd college ed. (Cleveland: William Collins & World Publishing, 1974), 317.

— CHAPTER 11 —

COME TO THE TABLE

Communion plays a vitally important part in the life of the believer. By partaking of the Communion Table, we recognize, celebrate, and identify ourselves with the death, burial, resurrection, ascension, and soon return of the Lord Jesus Christ. We should never forget the great sacrifice that God made in sending His Son to die for us or how Jesus willingly laid down His life for us.

This Table is significant and we should approach it with dignity, honor, reverence, and respect. But there are too many people in the modern Church who do not see this Table as a vital part of their worship. To them, Communion is nothing more than an archaic ritual with no real significance.

At some churches, taking Communion is treated as common. It's something that happens every time the doors are opened. In the Bible, Jesus didn't tell us how often to observe

Communion. He just said to do it in remembrance of Him. He allows us to choose when, where, and how we will partake. But we should never get to the point where Communion becomes commonplace and we lose sight of its meaning.

On the other hand, too many people only remember the death, burial, and resurrection of the Lord Jesus Christ once a year, at Easter time. Yes, it's important to celebrate Resurrection Sunday, but it's more important that we *continually* show forth the Lord's death until He comes by regularly partaking of Communion.

At RHEMA Bible Church, we celebrate Communion on the first Sunday of every month. But just because we partake of Communion so regularly doesn't mean that it should become a lifeless ritual or "just something that we do." If we're not careful, Communion can become a ritual void of the true meaning and blessing God intends for it to have in our life.

Really, unless we allow every one of our church services to be directed by the Holy Spirit, *every* service could become an empty ritual! We would come in, greet a few people, sing a few songs, pray, and listen to a message. Then we would shake hands with a few people and go home. Unfortunately, there are many people today who are doing just that. They're going through the motions, but they're not worshipping God with their whole heart. Each service should be full of life and that includes every Communion service.

The Communion table is a reminder that God has brought us into fellowship with Himself. God has invited us to come to the Communion Table because we are valuable and precious in

His sight. We are so valuable and precious to Him that He paid a high price to make it possible for us to accept His invitation.

Your Invitation to Fellowship With God

I like to think of the Communion Table as our invitation from God to come into His Presence. In effect, God is saying, "Come on in! Sit down and put your feet under My table and let's fellowship together."

1 JOHN 1:3,7

3 . . . our fellowship is with the Father and with his Son, Jesus Christ. . . .

7 But if we walk in the light, as he is in the light, we have fellowship with one another, and the blood of Jesus, his Son, purifies us from all sin.

As Christians, our fellowship is with God the Father, Jesus Christ, and our brothers and sisters in Christ. God *wants* to fellowship with us.

Have you ever been invited to a friend's house to eat? The invitation indicates that your friend thinks of you favorably and that he would like to share a meal with you. It means that he desires to fellowship with you and is willing to hear what you have to say. That invitation means that he will help you if you have a need and he is able.

Because God has invited us to His Table, we know that through Jesus we have been reconciled to God. We have been brought back into favor with Him. God reconciled us to

Himself through the blood of His Son Jesus. The blood made us worthy to be in God's Presence. God desires fellowship with us. He wants to hear what we have to say. And He stands ready, willing, and *able* to help us. A friend is limited and can help only if he is able, but God is *unlimited* and will *always* help!

The Table Has Been Set

Before Jesus went to the Cross, He prepared a table for His disciples, and by instituting the ordinance of Communion, He also prepared a table for you and me. Now by faith we can partake of everything God has provided for us.

PSALM 23:5

5 You prepare a table before me in the presence of my enemies. You anoint my head with oil; my cup overflows.

Each phrase of Psalm 23:5 has great significance. First, we see that God prepares a table before us and that He doesn't do it in secret. No! He prepares a table before us in the presence of our enemies so they, too, can see that God loves, protects, and provides for us!

But God doesn't stop there. Second, He anoints our heads with oil. Several Bible commentators note that it was customary in Eastern countries to pour oil on the head of an honored guest at a banquet. When we come to the Lord's Table, we are all honored guests. God considered us so valuable and wanted so much for us to sit at His Table that He sent His only Son to deliver a personal invitation.

This verse ends with God filling our cup to overflowing. God has given us the bottomless cup of salvation and blessings. His goodness and mercy toward us will never run out!

The Communion Table represents the love, care, concern, and commitment of our Heavenly Father. God loves and cares for His creation. And He demonstrated His concern for us and commitment to us by sending His only Son to die on the Cross that we might have everlasting life (John 3:16). God loves us enough to send His only Son. And Jesus loved us enough to lay down His life for us (John 10:18).

Through Christ's sacrificial death, God made a way to extract man from the chains of sin, sickness, poverty, and all the evils that the god of this world had afflicted upon God's creation.

2 CORINTHIANS 4:4
4 The god of this age has blinded the minds of unbelievers, so that they cannot see the light of the gospel of the glory of Christ, who is the image of God.

Why would anyone choose to remain a slave to sin rather than live free in relationship with God? Second Corinthians 4:4 says that Satan has blinded the minds of unbelievers.

God never intended that we suffer the things we endure in this world. If you'll study the beginning of mankind in the Book of Genesis, you'll discover that God created man to fellowship with Him and worship Him, but the enemy deceived man and stole him away.

God loved us so much that He didn't forget about us and create another race of people somewhere else to worship Him. Instead, He sent His only Son to redeem us.

God was so concerned about our welfare that He sent Jesus Christ to ensure that all the promises of God are available to us. Second Corinthians 1:20 says, *"For no matter how many promises God has made, they are 'Yes' in Christ. And so through him the 'Amen' is spoken by us to the glory of God."*

In the Midst of Trouble, Run *to* God!

The circumstances of life will always try to beat us down and rob us of the joy of our salvation. This is to be expected because God's enemy is Satan, the god of this age. John 10:10 says that the devil has come to steal, kill, and destroy. By stealing, killing, and destroying, Satan tries to beat people down and ruin as many lives as he can.

Jesus warned us about this. He told us that we will face trials and tribulations as long as we live in this world.

JOHN 16:33

33 "I have told you these things, so that in me you may have peace. In this world you will have trouble. But take heart! I have overcome the world."

No matter how much faith we have, we will face troubles in this world. Faith in God does not guarantee freedom from trials and troubles. But faith in God *does* guarantee that we will *triumph* over the trials and troubles that come our way. We can take heart, knowing that Jesus has overcome the world!

(Too many people try to misuse faith and make unscriptural "faith statements." If you want to study further what faith *is not,* you can read my book or listen to my audio series *Another Look at Faith.* In that teaching, I cover in greater detail the subject of faith—what it *is* and what it *is not.*)

When we're in the middle of a crisis situation, we need to be careful that we don't start questioning God's willingness to take care of us. To do so is a slap in God's face, so to speak. God has already demonstrated His willingness to always take care of us. He loved us, cared for us, was concerned about us, and was committed to us to the extent that He sent His only Son to die for us. We should never question whether God cares about us, given the great lengths to which He has already gone to demonstrate how much He cares.

Remember when the Israelites began to question God as they wandered in the desert? They questioned God because they forgot about His love, care, and concern for them. They began to doubt His commitment to them.

PSALM 78:18–19

18 They willfully put God to the test by demanding the food they craved.

19 They spoke against God, saying, "Can God spread a table in the desert?"

Psalm 78 details Israel's long history of rebellion against God. They put God to the test by demanding the food they craved.

The psalmist said the Israelites *spoke against God* when they asked if He was able to spread a table in the desert for them. God views our grumbling and complaining as unbelief. Even though God had already performed many miracles for the Israelites in the wilderness, they still doubted His faithfulness, power, and ability to provide.

Unfortunately, many Christians doubt God's goodness even though He has proven Himself over and over again. Many times when Christians find themselves in crisis situations, they turn away from God instead of coming to Him. When believers start questioning God's love and concern for them, they are speaking against God and His very nature.

1 JOHN 4:7–10

7 Dear friends, let us love one another, for love comes from God. Everyone who loves has been born of God and knows God.

8 Whoever does not love does not know God, because God is love.

9 This is how God showed his love among us: He sent his one and only Son into the world that we might live through him.

10 This is love: not that we loved God, but that he loved us and sent his Son as an atoning sacrifice for our sins.

God has proven His love for you in the most extreme way possible—by sending Jesus. And God has proven His love for you by the many blessings He has bestowed upon you and made available to you.

So if you find yourself in the middle of a crisis, instead of asking, "Can God?" you need to immediately proclaim the truth. You can boldly say, "Greater is He that is in me than he that is in the world; therefore, I am an overcomer through Christ Jesus" (1 John 4:4). You can boldly declare, "I can do all things through Christ who strengthens me" (Phil. 4:13 *NKJV*), or, "I always triumph in Christ Jesus" (2 Cor. 2:14). When you run up against an obstacle, test, or trial, immediately begin to speak in agreement with God, not against Him.

God has *already* prepared a table of blessing for you, so the "desert season" of life is not the time to question Him. Nor is it the time to stop assembling together with other believers. Times of crisis are when you should run *to* the Table and to the company of those who believe the way you do. Run to God, not away from Him, and experience the Table of blessings He has already prepared for you. That is your way out of the desert!

The Communion Table is a Table of deliverance. In fact, the Communion Table is set with whatever you need in order to live the abundant life God destined for you. God loved you enough to provide a Table of blessing for you, and the Table is laden with everything you could ever need or want. All you have to do is come to the Table!

The Communion Table speaks to us of how much God loves us and how willing He is to take care of us. The Table presents the Gospel of our salvation to us every time we partake. If we'll listen, we'll hear it speak to us of forgiveness, safety, preservation, deliverance, health, provision, and every other blessing God made available to us through Jesus.

At what we call the Last Supper, the table set for the 12 apostles spoke to them of the past, the present, and the future. The Communion Table speaks to us of these same things today. It declares to us that Jesus came. He died. He arose. And He's coming again! The Communion Table is still the table that speaks!

Why should you consider attending
RHEMA
Bible Training Center?

Here are a few good reasons:

- Training at one of the top Spirit-filled Bible schools anywhere
- Teaching based on steadfast faith in God's Word
- Growth in your spiritual walk coupled with practical training in effective ministry
- Specialization in the area of your choosing: Youth or Children's Ministry, Evangelism, Pastoral Care, Missions, or Supportive Ministry
- Optional intensive third-year programs—School of Worship, School of Pastoral Ministry, School of World Missions, and General Extended Studies
- Worldwide ministry opportunities—while you're in school
- An established network of churches and ministries around the world who depend on RHEMA to supply full-time staff and support ministers

Call today for information or application material.
1-888-28-FAITH (1-888-283-2484)
www.rbtc.org

RHEMA Bible Training Center admits students of any race, color, or ethnic origin.

OFFER CODE—BKORD:PRMDRBTC

Word Partner Club:

WORKING *together* TO REACH THE WORLD!

People. Power. Purpose.

Have you ever dropped a stone into water? Small waves rise up at the point of impact and travel in all directions. It's called a ripple effect. That's the kind of impact Christians are meant to have in this world—the kind of impact that the RHEMA family is producing in the earth today.

The *Word Partner Club* links Christians with a shared interest in reaching people with the Gospel and the message of faith in God.

Together we are reaching across generations, cultures, and nations to spread the Good News of Jesus Christ to every corner of the earth.

To join us in reaching the world, visit **www.rhema.org/wpc**
or call, 1-800-54-FAITH (543-2484)